MW00324132

"Rashawn Copeland takes the reader on a personal journey to experience the love of the Father—a wonderful book for anyone searching for home."

Eric Metaxas, *New York Times* bestselling author and host of the nationally syndicated *Eric Metaxas Radio Show*

"We don't have to impress, perform for, or prove ourselves to God, and Rashawn Copeland's life tells that story well. With a huge heart and deep conviction, *Start Where You Are* is a simple, straightforward anthem about the love God has for all of us, and Rashawn is a joyful guide pointing the way."

Emily P. Freeman, *Wall Street Journal* bestselling author of *The Next Right Thing*

"Compelling, poetic, and inspiring, Rashawn Copeland's *Start Where You Are* encourages us to embrace the greatest need in human life—a chance to start again, right where we are! I can't imagine someone picking up this book and regretting it. Rashawn is a passionate storyteller, sharing his painful and broken moments with fearless vulnerability."

Trent Shelton, founder of Rehab Time and author of *The Greatest You*

"Real, convicting, transparent. This book brings hope of a second chance, a clean slate, and divine appointments with a merciful God and invites you to grow deeper in your relationship with God and better understand His character. Rashawn writes with passion, vulnerability, and honest humor. The joy many see on his face is depicted in this book and is a result of God's sweet mercies!"

Alena Pitts, age thirteen, actress (*War Room*) and cousin of Priscilla Shirer

"For a guy who understands the feeling of being written off, Rashawn shares a fresh reminder on how Jesus says, 'I want him no matter how messy he is.' You may feel unworthy, useless, and upset; this book will push you to refocus your life and energy back on the Source of life, Jesus Christ. This isn't just a book. It's an invitation to God's best for your life. Start where you are and get excited about the outrageous role you can play in God's unfolding love story of grace and hope."

Darryl Strawberry, *New York Times* bestselling author, evangelist, and four-time World Series champ

"A refreshing encouragement. *Start Where You Are* has deep potential to bring healing and peace to those who are broken and hurting."

Carey Nieuwhof, bestselling author of *Didn't See It Coming* and founding pastor of Connexus Church

"*Start Where You Are* is filled with fresh hope for anyone who feels stagnant in their spiritual journey. The transparency and vulnerability of this book are refreshing and empowering. This book will meet every reader right where there are and right where they need it most!"

Bobby Gruenewald, founder of the YouVersion Bible app and innovation pastor of Life.Church

"*Start Where You Are* is a poetic, powerful, and practical book that opens our eyes to what it means to be love in a sometimes hateful world. My friend Rashawn gives truthful insights into the social trends of today and shares how God longs to meet us right there, on the ever-constant timelines of Tik-Tok and Twitter—and brings His timeless love that never changes. This book is a must-read we all need!"

Meredith Foster, author of *Fostering Your Best Self*, YouTuber, and influencer

"Rashawn Copeland writes from a place of deep conviction and touches lives in many ways. *Start Where You Are* is a call to celebrate God's love and mercy and move forward with Him out of our messy past. As Rashawn's friends, we joyfully recommend this book wholeheartedly."

Cole and Sav Labrant, influencers and authors of *Cole and Sav*

"Rashawn has an amazing story. I hope you will grab this incredible book."

Greg Laurie, pastor of Harvest Christian Fellowship, author, and founder of Harvest America

START WHERE YOU ARE

How God Meets You in Your Mess,
Loves You through It, and Leads You Out of It

Rashawn Copeland

BakerBooks

a division of Baker Publishing Group
Grand Rapids, Michigan

Published by Baker Books
a division of Baker Publishing Group
PO Box 6287, Grand Rapids, MI 49516-6287
www.bakerbooks.com

Library of Congress Cataloging-in-Publication Data
Names: Copeland, Rashawn, 1987– author.
Title: Start where you are : how God meets you in your mess, loves you through it, and leads you out of it / Rashawn Copeland.
Description: Grand Rapids, Michigan : Baker Books, [2020]
Identifiers: LCCN 2020003187 | ISBN 9781540900111 (paperback)
Subjects: LCSH: Christian life. | God (Christianity)—Love. | Copeland, Rashawn, 1987– | Clergy—United States—Biography.
Classification: LCC BV4501.3 .C67935 2020 | DDC 248.4—dc23
LC record available at https://lccn.loc.gov/2020003187

978-1-5409-0112-5 (hardcover)

The author is represented by MacGregor & Luedeke Literary.

Illustrations © 2020 by Emily Mills. Used by permission.

Some names and details have been changed to protect the privacy of the individuals involved.

TO MY DAD.

This book is for you because I
know God is calling you.
A yearning cry is reaching out from His
heart telling you to "Start where you are."
You taught me what it means to love and lead
a family, the importance of living a life of
integrity, and love that makes life worth living.
I love you more than words can say.
I'm so thankful to be Rodney Copeland's son.

Contents

7

Foreword

I will never forget where I came from. When my boxing career began to soar, my moral standards started to nosedive. I gave in to one too many temptations—and because of the heaviness of my sin I became shackled with shame. I found myself overwhelmed and overworked by great darkness with no sense of hope. Despite the glamour of the spotlight, I found myself quite often lost in the shadows of a lukewarm Christian life. Although I had strong drive and a noble dream, sadly God wasn't my priority. I went to church on Sunday morning, but by Monday night I was right back in my routine of getting drunk and gambling. I never took a moment to reflect on who I was hurting. *I was simply stuck in my mess.* I was immoral and drunk many nights before I ever felt any sorrow or remorse about it. I knew that none of it would ever satisfy the deepest longings of my soul. I just found myself more confused about what the true meaning of life was. Being one of the highest-paid athletes in the world in 2012 still didn't help light up the darkness in my soul. The old saying is true: money can't buy happiness.

Today, many of my fans would say my greatest victory of all time was versus Oscar De La Hoya. But that's not true at all. My greatest victory by far was when I accepted Jesus Christ as my Lord and Savior. God is using His unfailing mercy as a message through my life to help transform millions of lives.

I refused to be marked by the traumas of my past, deprivation, and the paralyzing mindset of poverty. *That is where I started.* In a culture that lays great stress on being self-reliant, wealthy, and powerful, God has reversed every human opinion on what significance truly is. *You can start with nothing at all.* Jesus came into our world as a helpless, vulnerable baby, and this is why you can have confidence you are not alone when you feel weak and vulnerable. Jesus came as a baby, and He will return as King to conquer and reign once and for all. All of your impossibilities are possible with God. No battle is too great for Him.

Right now, what's the biggest fight in my life? Honestly, it has nothing to do with the boxing ring. The biggest fight in my life is for people to be set entirely free to become who God is calling them to be. That's the good fight of faith. That's the fight that takes more endurance than twelve rounds in a boxing ring.

You might not realize it yet, but you aren't fighting alone. You are free to start over again with God by your side. And *Start Where You Are* holds a captivating message for every person on the face of the planet. Rashawn is a beloved brother in Christ. I felt compelled to be part of this project, because this message hits much harder than Floyd Mayweather. I'm not kidding! Rashawn has impacted thousands with the gospel on my home island of Mindanao, Philippines. He shares that a life lived intimately with God may not be the easiest. But it will always be the fullest, richest, and most exciting life possible not only now but in eternity.

When Rashawn and I first met, our conviction for the gospel immediately resonated around a shared passion for seeing people far from God moving closer to Him. We are both on a journey of learning more about the heart of God Almighty, but I can genuinely say we are on our way. We eagerly look to meet people where they are and make disciples all over the world for God's glory. This material is a product of patience and passion for seeing people saved, transformed, and propelled into God's purposes for their life. Rashawn has provided a simple, biblical, and practical book for anyone who has faced obstacles and needs help to overcome. I pray that God will use this book to highlight the love and mercy for us He demonstrated through His Son, Jesus, who will fuel your faith and strengthen your soul. After you start where you are, make sure you spread the message of Christ all over the world for God's glory.

Manny Pacquiao, fighter, servant, difference maker

pacquiaofoundation.org

Just Start Here

God is calling out to you.

Do you hear His voice?

Be still and listen.

Can you hear it?

Listen for the cry from God's heart, asking you to enter into the mystery of your life, the one He created for you to discover.

Do you know why you were made? Has anyone ever told you?

You were made to be blessed by God and sent to bless others. Consider the beauty of God's perfect plan. He longs to wrap you in His infinite love so you can spread His love to the whole world.

God doesn't just *want* this for you. You *need* this from Him. It's why you're alive.

What might happen if you really listened to His voice?

What if I became the person God created me to be?

What if I knew Jesus was fully invested in the details of my life?

What if I wholeheartedly believed Jesus was with me in each moment?

Imagine the difference all this would make! Take a few moments to picture it with me. Allow God's voice to flood your soul with love.

How does it feel?

What if you started each day like this? Can you imagine the possibilities?

I know what you're thinking. Life is busy, and you easily forget to invite the Lord into your daily affairs. I totally get it. I'm no spiritual master. No great religious leader. No church calls me their senior pastor. I'm just a guy who takes God seriously when He promises to be present in our lives. And I'm telling you, it makes all the difference. You can do it too.

I might be waiting in a doctor's office, nervous about impending test results. *I remember that He is with me. I take this truth seriously.* I might be in a hard conversation with my wife. *I remember that He is with me. I take this truth seriously.* I might be looking at my bank account, worried about next month's bills. *I remember that He is with me. I take this truth seriously.*

Peace comes, answers avail themselves, and hope reignites—not because I am special but because the Lord is so good and keeps His promises. Jesus is with us. But do we want to be with Him?

How would imagining Him with you reshape your days, especially the troubled ones? How might it transform your entire life?

Start Where You Are

The presence of Jesus doesn't always offer an immediate fix for our problems. Just because God is with us doesn't mean He'll change everything around us. God doesn't promise us an easy life. He promises us a *God-with-us* life. He will someday complete the good work He started in each of us. But our current circumstances might not change soon. Keep this in mind. Your financial burdens may not soon be lifted. Your health may continue to decline. Your estranged daughter might not call you back. Your problems won't be solved overnight. I'm not saying it's impossible. After all, we serve a God who makes the blind see and the lame walk! But most change comes over time.

Your problems, however long you may deal with them, can be seen differently if you understand that God's heart is wide open to you, as you are, all of the time. As you read these pages, open your heart to God's open heart so you can see how big God's dreams are for you.

Open your heart—even if you don't believe in God. Even if you hate God. Give God a chance. Trust me, once you experience the reality of God's love in your life, nothing is the same.

Start where you are.

Start with addiction.

Start with pornography.

Start with pride.

Start with fear.

Start with infidelity.

Start with shame.

Start with guilt.

Start with anxiety.

Start with depression.

Start with doubt.

Start with jealousy.

Start with suicidal thoughts.

Start with weariness.

Start with loneliness.

Start with comparison.

You are not stuck where you are. You can turn it all over to Jesus. All of it. If you start where you are, God will take you where you need to be.

Come Up, Go In, Reach Out

We serve a God who ordered every nook and cranny of creation. Our God is a master architect, and everywhere we look we see evidence of His perfect designs. Woven into the very fabric of Jesus's life and ministry is a pattern we can also follow. Consider the three movements of the kickstart to Jesus's ministry: he gets baptized, he gets tempted in the desert, and then he goes out to do ministry.

1. He comes up.
2. He goes in.
3. He reaches out.

At Jesus's baptism by John the Baptist in the Jordan River, God sends the Holy Spirit to empower Him. Before Jesus begins to formally go about His Father's work, He must receive everything He needs from the Father. He knows there is only one Source with enough strength for His work, and Jesus comes up to that Source in a spiritual way just as He is physically "coming up" out of the water. He's asking for everything God has. He comes up out of the water knowing the Father will give Him everything He needs. The Bible says, "As Jesus was coming up out of the water, he saw heaven being torn open and the Spirit descending on him like a dove. And a voice came down from heaven: 'You are my Son, whom I love; with you I am well pleased'" (Mark 1:10–11). In this moment, Jesus comes up to God and is given everything He needs: God's Spirit and affirmation of eternal love. We too can begin each and every day with this first step. We Come Up to God, trusting He will give us everything we need to be blessed and bless others.

After we Come Up, we must take time to Go In. Right after Jesus is baptized, the Holy Spirit sends Him into the desert for a period of forty days, where He is tempted by Satan. We're also told God sends angels to attend to Him the entire time (vv. 12–13). Jesus fasts and prays, and He experiences that the power of God's Holy Spirit and Scripture are enough to ward off any temptations Satan can throw His way. By "going in," Jesus internalizes what God gave Him when He "came up" at His baptism. In the desert He comes to understand that He has everything He needs for the coming journey. It's not enough that we merely Come Up to God to receive briefly from Him. We must then spend time praying, studying His Word, and fellowshiping with the Holy Spirit to solidify God's truth in us.

We Go In, but we can't stay in forever. Eventually, we must follow the example of Jesus and Reach Out into the world. Jesus wastes no time getting started. He immediately proclaims the good news of God, saying, "The time has come. . . . The kingdom of God has come near. Repent and believe the good news!" (v. 15). Just after His first sermon, He goes down to the Sea of Galilee and picks up His first disciples, Simon and Andrew, two fishermen whose lives He turns upside down. "'Come, follow me,' Jesus said, 'and I will send you out to fish for people'" (v. 17). The disciples are invited to follow His pattern. So are we. Jesus promised to make them fishers of people, and He offers us the same promise. And, like any master of order, He'll complete His work.

– – – – – – – –

It's a simple pattern. We come up to go in to reach out. Each chapter of this book will flow through these movements. Allow the structure to help you see where you are in your journey. When we Come Up, God meets us in our mess. When we Go In, God loves us through our mess. When we Reach Out, God leads us beyond our mess.

Let's get started.

1

From Dirty to Worthy

Just As We Are

When my son Jerrell was a youngster, my brother Mashawn would bring him to my college football games. After one game, Jerrell was playing in the dirt beneath the stands when I ran over with an ice-cold freezie I'd bought for him. He loved these treats—most of the time, he liked the treat better than the game he came to watch. But this time his mouth was so full of dirt he couldn't even drink the freezie!

That's how we are with God and His gifts. He wants to give us good things, but we settle for dirt. The good news is our behavior doesn't affect God's desire to give us good gifts anyway. Likewise, I didn't leave dirt in Jerrell's mouth, because I loved him too much for that. I picked him up, washed out his mouth, and gave him the freezie. That's what love does. And that's who God is: love (1 John 4:8). God is also a good father (Rom. 8:15). We are His children, and He never fails to treat us as a loving father would, giving us the good things we need. As Paul says, God has prepared things for us that are so much greater than we can imagine (1 Cor. 2:9). God wants to cleanse us of all the dirt we've been playing around in—be it anger, religion, jealousy, pride, or lust. But we have to allow God to get us out of the dirt. So many of us are too ashamed to ask for this love because we think our dirt is too dirty for God. But as Bob Goff says, "If you think your mess-up is bigger than God's grace, that's your second mistake."[1]

God loves us perfectly and unconditionally simply because He made us. Nothing we do can diminish this undeniable, unexplainable, unthinkable, unspeakable love!

Even if we ignore Him, disrespect Him, or reject Him.

God's love endures forever.

You are not too broken for God to fix.

You are not too dirty for God to cleanse.

You are not too far for God to reach.

You are not too guilty for God to forgive.

You are not too worthless for God to love.

God loves you right where you are.

For I am convinced that neither death nor life, neither angels nor demons, neither the present nor the future, nor any powers, neither height nor depth, nor anything else in all creation, will be able to separate us from the love of God that is in Christ Jesus our Lord. (Rom. 8:38–39)

God doesn't grade on a curve but on a cross. No matter how broken or brilliant, young or old, we are invited by Jesus to come and lay our lives down at the foot of His cross. And there, in the mysterious workings of His sacrifice, our old selves are made new.

God uses all circumstances for His purposes and glory. David was one of the greatest men of God in the Bible. He was also one of the worst sinners. David wrote most of the poems in the Old Testament book of Psalms. In Psalm 139:16, he says this about God: "All the days ordained for me were written in your book before one of them came to be." All the days. Not just our best days but also our worst days. Even though we may feel unworthy, we have to believe that nothing we've done can change the reality that God created us out of His deep love.

You are not dirty. You are worthy. David was a great king, but he was also a murderer and adulterer. And yet the Bible calls him a man after God's own heart (1 Sam. 13:14). David came up to God in the midst of his mess, and God wanted him to come just as he was.

We Come Up to Be Changed

God accepts us as we are but loves us too much to let us stay there. Good fathers don't let their children eat dirt when they have something better to give them. Good fathers meet their children in their mess so they can guide them out of it. God helped humanity out of its mess through the life, death, and resurrection of Jesus. The Bible says, "God demonstrates his own love for us in this: While we were still sinners, Christ died for us" (Rom. 5:8). This passage says nothing about what we need to do in order to receive God's love. It says *He* did this—while we were still sinners. God did the work before we acknowledged our need for it.

Before I welcomed God's love into my life I worried a lot about death. I fretted over what I needed to do to avoid going to hell. I had no idea where to start. *What "fix" will make God love me enough to bring me to heaven? Which rules should I follow? How often do I need to go to church?*

It wasn't until I heard the good news of Jesus Christ stated simply that I learned the process was itself quite simple: I just had to repent (aka be genuinely remorseful about my sins and joyfully turn away from my mess)! Repent in order to receive God's best for my life. Declare Jesus as Lord and believe God brought Him back from the dead. Boom! Nothing more and nothing less.

The gospel is a precious gem to be cherished not because I had to "Find Jesus" but because "Jesus found *me*."

The Bible says that if we sincerely believe the good news of Jesus, we will be saved from eternal separation from God and will enjoy being forever united with the God of the universe.

Maybe this is the first time you're hearing the good news. Or maybe you've heard it before but thought it too good to be true. Either way, you're hearing it now and have the opportunity to respond in faith. Receive God's free gift, come just as you are, and be made into who you were meant to be.

GO IN

We Go In Honestly

One of the best ways to respond to God is to just talk to Him—to pray. Talking to God isn't as hard as you might think. God loves our imperfect prayers. Jesus criticizes people who say long, fancy prayers to impress others (Matt. 6:5) and says we should call upon our Father in heaven using whatever honest words we have. God is less concerned with our vocabulary than the condition of our hearts. All God wants when we pray is a "broken spirit" and a "contrite heart" (Ps. 51:17).

Genuine prayer is all about sharing our problems and pain with God. The most important thing is that we come to Him *not* as who we wish we were but as we actually are: broken and sinful. Our prayers don't have to feel spiritual; they can simply be whatever is on our hearts and minds. All God wants is authenticity.

If I'm worried about my job, then God wants to hear about my job. If it's my marriage that's under stress, then God wants to hear about that. At its best, prayer is the heart overflowing into the mouth. Max Lucado said, "Our prayers may be awkward. Our attempts may be feeble. But since the power of prayer is in the One who hears it and not the one who says it, our prayers do make a difference."[2] God always hears the prayers that flow from a sincere heart. Your concerns may seem unimportant to the rest of the world, but every word, every syllable, every breath matters to Him.

Are you able to believe Jesus is the Lord of your life, that He came back from the dead, and that you can come to Him in honest prayer? It's okay if you're *not* okay. You can be angry, broken, doubtful, anxious, and overwhelmed. Jesus loves you whether or not you have faith in Him yet. He ain't afraid of your dirt!

I want to tell you more about King David. He was a special man with extraordinary gifts. What made him special wasn't his talent but the radical honesty he displayed before God. No matter what condition his heart was in, he courageously brought it to God in prayer through his psalms. He told God how he truly felt. Many of these psalms are about so-called "unspiritual" things. They aren't lofty prayers about the welfare of the world but the inner workings of David's heart and life, which were sometimes very dark. Here are just a few examples of his honest words:

- I have many enemies (Ps. 3:1).
- I cried aloud (3:4).

- I was in distress (4:1).
- Consider my groaning (5:1).
- I am languishing (6:2).
- My bones are troubled (6:2).
- My soul is greatly troubled (6:3).
- I'm weary from my groaning (6:6).
- I flood my bed with tears (6:6).
- See my affliction (9:13).
- There's sorrow in my heart all day (13:2).
- I find no rest (22:2).
- I am lonely and afflicted (25:16).
- The troubles of my heart are enlarged (25:17).
- I cried to You for help (30:2).
- I plead for mercy (30:8).
- Rescue me speedily (31:2).
- You have seen my affliction (31:7).
- You have seen the distress of my soul (31:7).

David understood that Going In is not just about asking God for things but pouring our hearts and souls out to Him. He knew that we're not allowed just to talk to God; we can groan and cry and scream if we need to. How beautiful it is to have a God who loves all of us—not only the beauty of what we show on the outside but the dark of what we hide on the inside.

God is at work in the messy middle. That's the miraculous message of the Bible. That's why it's not the prettiest book on your bookshelf. It's a sacred book filled with cracked characters. Its pages overflow with flawed people in need of a flawless God. The biblical writers never once edited out the flaws of their heroes.

God clothed in His majesty longs to meet you in your mess. He's working in your tears.

Brave Again

Going In means looking inside, and looking inside can be hard. I feel sick when I look into my messy past. For the longest time I desperately sought the approval of other people. The only time I felt good was when I wore a nice outfit and had a sharp haircut. If I didn't have it all together, I didn't even want to think about stepping foot outside.

During my senior year of high school, I signed with a D1 team to play football in college. I thought this was the breakthrough—the prestige would solve all of my problems! Spoiler alert: it didn't. As long as I needed success and acceptance from others to be okay, I was doomed. It was only when I realized that trusting in Jesus guaranteed rejection from the world that I finally found peace within myself. We can stop worrying about what we lack and know that His acceptance is all we need. Then we can stop getting stuck in the mess of our past and start seeing the possibility of our future.

Jesus never asked us to crave security. We are saved to be brave. No matter what we're facing right now, God is in complete control. That doesn't mean we can't feel afraid. But it does mean we shouldn't be controlled by fear. The truth of God's love is not that He will prevent bad things from happening but that He won't abandon us to them.

We spend a crazy amount of time remembering our failures even though God sent Jesus to let us know we are forgiven. Where we see failure to win, God sees a new future. Where we see rejection, God sees redirection. Where we allow our mess to define us,

God uses our mess to refine us. Don't be afraid to Go In; it's there, inside, where God gives us the courage to go out and accomplish all He has called us for. We can stop trying to figure this mess of a life out all on our own as we learn how to rely entirely on Him every step of the way.

✚ REACH OUT

Where God's Love Leads

Jesus spends forty days Going In while in the wilderness and wrestling with temptation from the devil. You'd think the guy would take a vacation after that. Instead, He dives headlong into ministry! We have to imagine Jesus had some doubts and insecurities about what He was getting Himself into. After all, saving the world is no small task, not even for the Son of God! The angels that attended to Him in the desert would continue to be with Him as He went throughout Galilee and Judea, but I wonder if He had any leftover fear from His time in the desert? Even though He didn't succumb to any of Satan's temptations, I wonder if He felt fragile. We can't know. What we know is that Jesus went out regardless of His feelings; He understood He was worthy because His Father in heaven said He was. Our heavenly Father says the same thing about us: we are not dirty, we are worthy!

I have to remind myself of that truth all the time. I don't know about you, but sometimes I wonder why God is so committed to loving us through our mess. Why would the God who created the vast, jaw-dropping, heart-pounding universe love us like His children?

Maybe it's because He's had His heart broken before?

God created a perfectly harmonious universe, free from shame and rejection, beautiful beyond what we can imagine. But Adam and Eve accepted the seductive bribes of Satan, bit into the forbidden fruit, and broke God's heart. In His infinite wisdom, God understood that we too would choose sin and death instead of His love. This is why He graciously sent His Son, Jesus, to restore His original design for us.

God's grace is sufficient for your past, your present, and your future. God's grace carried you to this very moment and will carry you on to whatever He has for you. Where God's grace goes, His love flows. You may have given up on Him, but He will never give up on you. He knows you, and He designed you for a life of significance. Take a moment to embrace the radical hope that you have been given in Jesus.

Nothing about this mess of a universe will ever make sense until you confront sin and recognize your desperate need for God's forgiveness. My prayer is that you won't run from Him but will turn and run straight into His love. God has given you a friend who will stick closer to you than a brother. His name is Jesus. Give Him a chance and you'll see the Lord is good. Don't fall for the lie that says God doesn't care about you. It isn't easy to believe in a God who has allowed so many people to break your heart. I get that. But don't forget that His heart has been broken too. And even in that heartbreak, He reaches out to you. With His strength, you can Reach Out to others too.

Refined for His Glory

You may think, *I'm too broken to reach out.* Believe it or not, God's purposes will be accomplished through your struggles. There's a blessing in the midst of the adversity of rejection. Like nothing else, the humbling pain of rejection can redirect us toward restoration if we allow it to usher us into the presence of God. For it's only there—with Him—that all things become possible. Jesus put it this way: "Apart from me you can do nothing" (John 15:5). You may not be able to see that from where you are now, but picture yourself in a thousand years. On that day, God's love will by far have surpassed every momentary affliction you have faced, because God promises to complete the good work He has begun in us (Phil. 1:6). His love will be revealed in spite of our pain and suffering just as it was for Jesus, who suffered the cross before being raised to glory with the Father.

The Bible isn't a rule book; it's a love letter. It's the story of God's heart for His people. In this letter we learn God loves us so much He was willing to send His Son to reach out to us and to suffer with and for us so that nothing we experience in this life will be in vain. God raised Jesus from the dead, and He will do the same for us if we trust in Him. We can boil the whole Bible down to a single verse, John 3:16, which says: "For God so loved the world that he gave his one and only Son, that whoever believes in him shall not perish but have eternal life."

This is the hopeful heart of the Bible: the man upstairs came downstairs so that we wouldn't have to live in the basement forever. God reached out to us. John 3:16 is the verse I turn to when I need to be reminded that God has made a way for all of us to come back to Him. Because of our sin, we deserved to die on the cross, not Jesus. We are the villain and Jesus is the hero. In other stories, the hero takes down the villain, but this story has the hero dying *for* the villain.

We must keep our eternal destiny in mind and refuse to allow the broken experiences of our lives to define our worth. God created us in His image to rejoice in and reveal His glory to the world. But we cannot do that when our pain defines us. We must be defined instead by His perfect image in us and the divine purpose for which He created us: to bring Him glory and bless others through the love He has freely poured out for us.

Have you accepted this divinely orchestrated identity and purpose for your life? Can you accept that the mess of your past doesn't come close to the immeasurable weight of God's love for you? It's true. His love makes you worthy—just as you are, right where you are.

TAKING THE NEXT STEP

PAUSE AND PONDER

You are fully seen and known as you are. You are fully accepted and loved as you are. But you are never left where you are. Remain confident in the transformative truth that God is personally and passionately committed to your good, even when you fail.

PRESS INTO PRAYER

God's infinite love is closer than you think.
Take a breath and know this is true.
Seriously. Breathe in. Now breathe out. The breath of life is an ever-present sign of God's love for you. That last inhale and exhale you took were His gift to you. Through the wonderful gift of breath—which God gives to us each moment—we catch a glimpse

of what true love is. Ever present and everlasting. Take another breath. Now go to Him in prayer.

Lord,

Place me where I'll grow the most. Teach me to love wherever I am planted. But help me to delight in You, not the dirt. Change me. Give me eyes that see the golden threads in my pain. Let me be a lighthouse in this valley. Have Your way today.

PROVE TO BE A PRACTICAL PIONEER

Who could you lavish with God's love today?

What would happen if the three words "God Loves Me" became the theme for your day?

START HERE

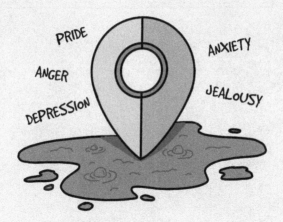

2

Where I Started

Pride is like bad breath. You don't know when you have it, but everyone else can smell it.

FRANCIS CHAN

They will betray their friends, be reckless, be puffed up with pride, and love pleasure rather than God.

2 TIMOTHY 3:4 NLT

⬆ COME UP

I'm in Los Angeles, the City of Angels, when an actual angel on Facebook saves my life. I'm vacillating between rage and despair, considering a walk down the hall to grab a gun and end my life. It wouldn't be hard. Just one pull of the trigger. I've been shot before. I know the havoc a bullet can wreak on the human body.

I also know I should stay in my room and go to bed. Tomorrow is a new day. Maybe my problems won't seem so bad in the light of a sunny Southern California morning. But maybe not. I walk down the hall, get the gun, and walk back to my bedroom.

No one else is home. No one will stop me.

My life looks fabulous from the outside. I'm living in a house my management team pays for, riding the rocket of internet fame in Hollywood, and working as a hype man for Soulja Boy. The money is great, the parties are incredible, and the women are incomparable. What more could a young, narcissistic twenty-something want out of life? Apparently *a lot*. Despite my worldly success, my spirit is miserable.

I thought money would fix it. It didn't. I thought the right woman would fix it. She didn't. I thought a Mercedes G Wagon would fix it. It didn't. There *has* to be more to life, but I don't know what it is. I've spiraled all the way into deep depression.

I put the gun barrel in my mouth and my entire body starts to shake. My mind races back to the night I was shot twice in the leg. I think of the twenty minutes I spent lying in an empty parking lot, weaving in and out of consciousness, before a stranger found me and took me to the ER. I worry this bullet won't kill me. I cannot handle that kind of pain again. I pull the gun out of my mouth and lay it down on the bed.

I put it back in my mouth.

I take it out again.

I reach for my phone.

Facebook is the first app I see. Absentmindedly, I click on the familiar blue and white icon and there it is: the post that saves my life. I only followed one Christian on Facebook. Her name was Genessis, and I'd met her once at a party after a Baylor football game in Waco. We spent the entire night talking. Genessis was different from the kind of woman I usually talked to in LA. She wasn't looking around, worried about whether there was someone more important she could talk to. She made eye contact when we spoke. She didn't check her phone incessantly. She was present. She was interested in me as a person. She didn't care about fame and money. She had values. I listened intently as Genessis told me about her faith. It was one of the best conversations I'd ever had. Eventually, the party ended, we friended each other on Facebook, and I flew back to LA. But now Genessis was back, speaking powerfully through a Facebook post in my darkest hour. She quoted the Bible:

> For I am convinced that neither death nor life, neither angels nor demons, neither the present nor the future, nor any powers, neither height nor depth, nor anything else in all creation, will be able to separate us from the love of God that is in Christ Jesus our Lord.[1]

Below the verse she explained that God's love is fully available to anyone who calls upon Him. *Anyone? Really?*

I read her post again. Then I read it again and again and again. I fall onto my face before God. I need to find out if what Genessis wrote was true. I pour my heart out to God and weep as I unload my heavy soul to the Lord. He receives me with a love I'll spend the rest of this book trying to explain, and how I feel makes me think of this quote attributed to St. Augustine: "In my deepest wound I saw your glory, and it dazzled me."

I forget all about the gun.

Genessis was right. God loved me, and nothing I had done could separate me from that love. I didn't deserve it. I hadn't earned it. But I had it. It was the best news I'd ever received.

The rest of my night wasn't easy. You don't go from the brink of suicide to sunshine and daisies over the span of a few hours. Like Jacob, I wrestled with God all night long, questioning and crying but ultimately accepting His vast love for me. By sunrise the next morning I knew a new life was also dawning.

Within days of my conversion, I returned home to Oklahoma with nothing but a heart full of new possibilities. I didn't know where I was going but I knew where to start: right where I was.

I had gone up to God. Now it was time to Go In to myself.

Starting Over

If we want God to change us through our mess, we have to be vulnerable enough to let Him in. We need to acknowledge where we are even if it's not where we want to be. But we don't stop there. God wants to take us somewhere better. But to believe that, we have to get real. We can't walk into the reality of God's plan for our lives if we're being dishonest with ourselves. Transparency with ourselves, others, and God is paramount.

Allow me to go first.

Growing up, I never even thought about working a nine-to-five job. From the moment I first touched a football, I knew I was special. By my sophomore year of high school I had a mailbox full of scholarship offers from top programs across the country. On the first play from scrimmage during my varsity season, I took the ball for a fifty-seven-yard touchdown. I was destined for NFL stardom.

And I might have been, but for the night a wannabe gangster shot me twice in the leg. Not that it was all his fault. My own stupidity played a role. Nobody forced me to meet him in an empty parking lot to defend the honor of the girl I had just started dating. I should have blown him off. Instead I allowed my pride to lead me into a dangerous situation—something pride is great at doing, by the way. Next thing I knew, two searing hot bullets pierced my leg and I was lying alone in a parking lot experiencing a pain beyond description. I survived and recovered quickly, but my football career never did. After I was shot, the major programs withdrew their offers because nobody wants guys on the roster who have been involved in gang violence. I barely made it to a junior college squad. From there I worked hard, transferred a few times, and eventually made it to the University of Kansas before transferring back down to a Division II school where I had a few good seasons. But it was nothing close to what I'd expected when I was a sophomore. There would be no NFL stardom for me.

That was a tough pill for me to swallow. You've probably had to abandon a dream too, and it's not an easy thing to do. Envisioning my life without football was impossible. Football was all I had ever known. There was no backup plan. Instead of using the time in college to take advantage of being at a great school that offered me multiple paths toward a prosperous future, I chose instead to fan the flame of personal frustration, which quickly led to depression. I coped with my difficulties by numbing my pain with weed, alcohol, and pursuing women.

I thought partying would work, or at least help, but it made me miserable. I reveled in the moments of escape but that's all they were: moments. As soon as the sex ended or the high wore off, I was right back where I started. I continued in vain attempts to fill the hole in my heart with anything and everything I could get my hands on, completely unaware that my heart would never be satisfied until I allowed it to rest in Jesus. But it was going to take some time before I came to believe that everlasting truth. In the meantime, I got smacked upside the head with another truth: fatherhood.

I know what you're thinking. *Hold up, Rashawn. Fatherhood?! You forgot to tell us about falling in love, getting married, and choosing to settle down with the love of your life.* I didn't forget. That's not how it went down—not the first time, anyway. I've since had two children with my wife. But back then I wasn't married; I slept with a friend and she got pregnant. I was sleeping around a lot then, something I'm not proud of. I wasn't ready to be a father. The thought of raising a child terrified me. I love my son so much and can't imagine my life without him. But still, those were confusing, dark days for me. Looking back now, I see my son is another reminder that God redeems all things. It may not have been the best decision for me to sleep with my friend, but God blessed my life with a beautiful son. I'm not advocating premarital sex. I'm saying that God works in mysterious ways, and we should never assume that what appears to be a bad situation will be a bad situation forever. God works for the good of all those that love Him (Rom. 8:28). I wasn't ready to be a father, but God, the perfect Father, allowed me to become the father my son needed.

A New Mission

Not long after I found out my son Jerrell was on the way, I also learned that one of my dearest childhood friends, JC, had died from suicide. JC fought hard against the terrible disease of depression. I felt awful for him and his family, but I also felt guilty because I'd known JC was struggling and had rebuffed his final attempts to connect with me. He reached out to me on Facebook

Messenger on multiple occasions. He wasn't asking for much. He just wanted to talk, but I didn't really take the time. Sometimes I'd reply and chat for a minute or two, but mostly I minimized or ignored his messages. I was too caught up in my own affairs to take time out of my day for a friend who needed me. Recently I considered pulling up our old message thread but couldn't bring myself to do it because I was too ashamed by what I knew I'd find there. Or by what I knew I *wouldn't* find there. Would it have made a difference if I'd replied to his messages? I'll never know.

JC reached out online, which is the least intrusive way a person can reach out, and still I did nothing. That haunts me. I wish I could travel back in time and reply to JC. But I can't. What I can do, however, is reply to the next person in pain who reaches out to me. JC's death is one of the main reasons I've dedicated my life to online ministry. The age of social media has brought with it plenty of trouble, no doubt, but what is often overlooked is how much kingdom work can be done with it. In mere seconds we can reach out to and connect with each other in ways that used to be impossible. Imagine if Paul could have sent a text message to Timothy when he was trying to get the early church off the ground. Imagine the difference that could have made! *We* have that opportunity. We can listen to and lift one another up, in real time, regardless of where we are in the world. What a blessing!

Between JC's death and Genessis's lifesaving Facebook post, God revealed my mission field to me. He's enabled me to minister to millions online through various Facebook pages, podcasts, and even directly on my phone via a text message service where people from all over send me prayer requests. It's unbelievable, as God's plans so often are.

On the night I almost took my life in LA, when I was on the floor, begging God to save me, I noticed a suitcase under my bed I hadn't previously seen. Desperate and curious, I opened it. Guess what was inside?

A Bible.

I'm not even joking.

I spent the entire night reading the words of Jesus and savoring God's amazing love and grace. The next day I walked to the bus station with that same Bible and bought a ticket back to Oklahoma. I was ready to surrender my dreams and embrace the new one God had for me. I had Gone In. Soon it would be time to Reach Out.

⊕ REACH OUT

It took time, but eventually I got back on my feet. Some close friends of mine got me plugged into a church where I was discipled and learned more about Jesus. Before my Hollywood days, I had been an officer in the Army. Once I got back to Oklahoma, I went back into the service. Soon after I also got a job in a local prison working as a guard. This job was the launching point of my ministry. In that jail, God taught me to be an evangelist.

This is when I first began to write little notes of encouragement and slide them into the inmates' cells. It was never really a conscious decision I made, just something God told me to do. I became known as the prison guard who liked to spread the good word. Eventually I wrote so many of these I collected them into a book I gave to the prisoners. It wasn't a masterpiece by any means, just a tool God used to spread His love. It was only a matter of time before I took these evangelistic efforts online. Until then my online presence had been solely about promoting myself. Now it was about Jesus.

START with PRIDE, END with GOD'S PURPOSE

But evangelizing online was problematic. There was a lot of content from my past I wanted to forget. Stuff I didn't want people seeing anymore, pictures of me partying and doing all kinds of things that wouldn't help make Jesus famous. I considered deleting everything. But as I prayed, God told me it would be more helpful to others if I left it all up. No filter. So that's what I did. To this day, you can go online and see a very different version of Rashawn Copeland. It's not a version I'm proud of, but it's who I once was. I thank the Lord He accepts us for all we are and have been, not just who we will become.

As I evangelized, I experienced His presence in ways I never imagined possible. I couldn't help but share God with my friends, my family, and the world. I leaned hard into social media, building upon the strong following I established in LA. I even decided to post my phone number. Anyone could call me. I wanted to speak with people all over the world about Jesus. I had no great skill to offer. I simply made myself available to anyone who needed me. I would post tweets and Facebook messages letting people know I was listening and praying. I discovered my life's passion and God's plan for my life: to walk alongside others in their darkest hours.

So that's where I started: in a dark bedroom in LA, thinking of ways to kill myself. I confronted my issues, and God redeemed my darkest moments, then called me to seek His mission for my life.

Where are you today?

Maybe you're where I was that night in LA, shaking and terrified, wondering if you're loved or if you have any future. Or maybe you're tight with Jesus but unclear about what He wants you to do next. Wherever you are, Jesus will not only meet you there but also help you meet others with His love. Jesus is never too caught up to reply to our messages. And He isn't turned off by how messy our mess is. Jesus transforms our mess into a message. When we're on the rocks, He's ready to show us He is *the rock*. We can do it right now. And we should—because right now is all we have. We all know tomorrow isn't guaranteed, but today is the day life can change forever.

Start where you are. It's not just merely about leaving your mark in the world; it's about living for the mark that has already been made by God through His Son, Jesus. Never allow yourself to sink in the moment of your mess. If you haven't been moving toward God, start now. Dedicate your life to knowing and loving Jesus so you can discover the amazing purposes He has for your life. He wants to bless you so you can then go and bless the world, making everything and everyone around you different.

TAKING THE NEXT STEP

PAUSE AND PONDER

God's love is fully available to anyone who calls upon Him.

PRESS INTO PRAYER

The second we allow the tough moments to become
 monuments,
we have lost sight of the Master of our moments.

The moments of chaos,
the days where it feels
as if our lives are
falling apart. Things
may just be coming together.
Where there is pain,
there is purpose.

Where there is war,
there is peace.
Where there's a start,
there is a finish.

Start now and finish with God,
and you will finish well in all that you do.

Lord,

You heard my cry! I thank You for allowing my pride to lead me into some deep and dirty places. Without them I wouldn't have felt Your mercy nor found my purpose. If it wasn't for my lowest of lows, I would've never found the Rock that is higher than I. You saved my life and gave me life. I'm so glad You heard my cry. Help me to trust in the sufficiency of Christ's power, not mine. Amen!

PROVE TO BE A PRACTICAL PIONEER

Take the time to respond to someone in pain. Ask God to show you who.

3

Peace

Peace I leave with you; my peace I give you. I do not give to you as the world gives. Do not let your hearts be troubled and do not be afraid.

JOHN 14:27

The Key that unlocks the treasure chest of God's peace is faith in God's promises.

JOHN PIPER

COME UP

A Voice in the Night

Everywhere I go—the plaza, the grocery store, Chick-fil-A—I can't help but notice that people are riddled by anxiety. I watch them and remember the years I spent frantically trying and failing to find peace. I hated that I didn't have the power to make my life more peaceful.

Ever been there? Have you ever asked, *Where is the peace I've been promised in the Lord?* I know men and women of all ages, races, and backgrounds who have asked that question. The way we wander anxiously about the world, unsure of where we can go to find peace, reminds me of the way I wandered around the woods when training for service in the Army. If you've spent any time in the woods, you know it's easy to get lost out there. When you don't know where you're going, panic sets in fast. Especially at night. On more than one occasion, I found myself hopelessly lost, wondering if I'd ever find my way out.

Imagine yourself in the woods at night. No iPhone. No compass. No map. Very little water and no food. It's starting to get cold. Branches crackle behind you. You turn around just in time to see a pair of shiny eyes disappear into the night.

How do you feel? Are you calm? Confident?

How about anxious?

Of course you're anxious! Nobody enjoys getting lost.

Now imagine a voice in the darkness calls your name. What would you do? Run away? Dive behind a tree and hope the voice goes away?

No way! You would sprint toward the voice that knows your name. Maybe the voice also knows the way out of the woods.

God calls our name in the midst of our anxiety. He says, "Incline your ear, and come to Me. Hear, and your soul shall live" (Isa. 55:3 NKJV). I think the "ear" the Bible is talking about here is the heart. God is calling out to us, offering a path to peace, but we can't hear Him if our hearts are not inclined to hear His voice.

Start with your anxiety. Come Up to God with everything—including the way you feel, especially when you feel anxious. Acknowledge the chaos around you but allow your heart to rest for a few moments and listen for the voice of Jesus. Can you hear

Him? He says, "Come to me, all you who are weary and burdened, and I will give you rest" (Matt. 11:28).

The path to peace is not found by stumbling upon it in the dark. It's found by responding to the voice calling out to us *from* the dark. Stop trying to find your way through the dark and respond to the voice calling your name. He knows the way out.

A Voice You Can Trust

I had already settled into my seat on the plane when my phone buzzed. It was a message from my wife. I just had time to look at it. Then I almost dropped my phone—I had to read Denisse's text twice to believe it.

> Rashawn, there's only $42 in the bank account.

> What happened?

> Rent happened. So did cell phone, seminary tuition, car payment, medical . . .

My heart sank as the plane taxied out to the runway. This trip to Grand Rapids had been planned for months. I was ready, but apparently my bank account wasn't. The anxiety set in. I was really upset. I mean . . . $42! That's not much.

> No bueno. This isn't good, hon. Well, I love you, and I will pray about it.

I set my phone on airplane mode and tried to get myself into prayer mode. Then I remembered I had forgotten to make a hotel reservation. "Lord," I prayed, "I could really use Your help right now." I thought about the car I had rented and wondered if it was big enough for me to sleep in. I had an important meeting the next day, and the thought of walking in without showering ratcheted up my anxiety to a whole new level. The flight was terrible.

Finally we landed—in a driving rainstorm. *Great*, I thought. *Things just keep getting better.* I had no money, no hotel, and now I would have no dry clothes. I was so stressed and frustrated. I'm usually the guy who never stops smiling, but this was more than I could handle.

"All right, God," I said. "You're in control."

Had I known my bank account was going to sink down to $42, I'd never have boarded that airplane. But I don't believe in happenstance. I believe in God's divinely orchestrated circumstance. He wanted me on that plane. Even though I had no idea what to do, God knew exactly what to do. So I did the only thing left for me to do: I trusted. I came up to God with no money and no plan, believing that the voice in the night was a voice I could trust.

As the plane taxied toward the gate, I did my best to take a child's posture toward my Good Father and be completely dependent upon Him. But after a few more minutes of listening to the rain pummel the fuselage, my anxiety was still skyrocketing. I had no idea what to do.

When I turned my phone back on, it flooded with notifications.

The first text I read was from my buddy Grant, who was scheduled to attend the same meeting as me the next day.

> My friend's parents are out of town, so we will have their house to ourselves!

You have to be kidding me, I thought. My anxiety was immediately replaced with gratitude. Once again, God provided when

I didn't deserve it. I deserved to sleep on the streets of Grand Rapids. Instead I was going to sleep in a comfy bed.

I slept so peacefully that night, overwhelmed by the blessings God had given me through the spontaneous generosity of strangers. I wish I'd felt that peace on the airplane. I wish I'd remembered that in chaos God is always calm.

The only times I lack peace are when I don't trust God enough. Jesus left us with peace. It is His peace that forever abides in us. The only question is whether or not we will trust it enough to live into it.

Instead of trusting God in chaotic circumstances, I often ask God to change my circumstances. But God wants us to ask for the faith that will take us *through* our circumstances. Job said, "Though He slay me, yet will I trust Him" (Job 13:15 NKJV). Jesus's disciples cried out, "Increase our faith!" (Luke 17:5). And when Daniel was thrown to the lions, he remained faithful to the Lord. That's the kind of faith I want to have! But this kind of faith requires believing God knows more than we do. We cannot have peace without trusting in God beyond the measure of our circumstances. My miracle on the plane didn't happen because of my faith—I wouldn't say I had much faith at all. The miracle happened because God is always in control.

⊙ GO IN

Don't Follow Your Heart

Life is confusing. For years, I lived in the middle of a contradiction. That's how my days chasing lights in Los Angeles all felt. Some days my soul ached, and I felt inconsolable. I was desperate to get beyond the anxiety, the emotional cloud of stress, the constant feeling that I was ruining my life. No matter how hard I tried, I just couldn't feel better. But the next day I'd feel totally different, smiling from ear to ear, the epitome of positivity. "I'm going to marry the most gorgeous, fashionable, hilarious woman. She will love me and I will love her forever!" I'd say. I believed it too. Until the next day.

I rode the ups and downs of this emotional roller coaster for a long time. The worldly advice to "Follow my heart" guided my steps. Nothing about that was stable. I swung back and forth between euphoria and desperation. I wanted fame and money, and the world told me to chase them down. But that's exactly how I hit rock bottom. I had everything my heart wanted: money, fame, and friends. Yet none of it brought me peace. To have real peace, I needed to Go In to God in prayer. I wasn't going to do that as long as I was following my own heart—I needed to follow His.

Once I finally escaped Los Angeles, came back home to Oklahoma, and started following after the Lord, He revealed a very important truth to me: my life isn't about me, it's about God and the work of His kingdom. As long as we only chase our hearts' desires and build our own micro-kingdoms, we remain hollow inside.

An empty heart is like a lifeless tomb in desperate need of God's resurrection power. The thing is, compared to the infinite wisdom of God, the opinion of our hearts and our human wisdom count for nothing. If human wisdom were enough, surely we would've solved all the world's problems by now. But Scripture tells us, "Those who trust in themselves are fools" (Prov. 28:26). Instead, we are told it is far better to "Trust in the LORD with all your heart, and lean not on your own understanding" (3:5).

Don't follow your heart. No matter what your dream is, it's not big enough to fill God's dream for your life. We must cast our crowns at His feet and surrender our castle for His kingdom. That's Going In. That's trading anxiety for peace.

Today I face the world with abiding joy because I'm not following my heart—I'm following God's desire for my heart. Big difference! I find meaning and purpose each day regardless of how I'm feeling. I'm part of something bigger now. Proverbs 19:21 says, "Many are the plans in a person's heart, but it is the LORD's purpose that prevails."

Peace over Comparison

If you're anything like me, you have to keep Going In to God to choose peace over anxiety. One morning, not long ago, I was with my lovely wife, Denisse. She was sipping coffee while I mentally prepped for the busy day ahead. I had social media content to create, meetings to attend, and phone calls to return. Without thinking, I opened Instagram to indulge briefly before the work of the day began. I started scrolling and saw friends and leaders I know, admire, and pray for. But then something tripped me up. Several friends had been invited to speak at a thriving youth camp I'd been dying to speak at, and I instantly felt envious. I kept scrolling. The envy grew. I started anxiously comparing myself to these people. *Why didn't the camp ask me? Am I not knowledgeable enough? Am I a bad public speaker? Do they doubt my authenticity?*

Can you see where this is going? I felt that what I had done wasn't good enough, which led to thinking *I* wasn't good enough. Nobody had given me this criticism. Nobody said, "Rashawn, you're not worthy." All that happened was I chose to compare myself with others instead of trusting who I am in God. When you look online before you look inline, your life will be out of line.

Several weeks later, I found myself back on social media, but this time, thank God, I came across a post by Louie Giglio that really spoke to me. Louie wrote:

A note to young leaders:
What's durable trumps what's visible. So often we are tempted to go for what looks good over what is good. Conditioned by an instant culture, the approval of others and a climate of comparison, we can lose ourselves in the quest to be seen, when the goal is to be steady. Don't get in too big a rush to tell the world what you know. Get to know the One who is unseen and walk with Him as if you really believe He is the best treasure of all. Work diligently toward the mission He calls you to, embracing the reality that what you do in secret will be rewarded in the open. Go from acceptance, not for acceptance. From approval, not for it.[1]

Louie was perfectly describing our need to Go In to God before we attempt to change the world. How needed are those words in today's social *me*-dia age? God hasn't made us to be scorekeepers, constantly comparing ourselves to others. Think of it this way: we were made to look vertically before we look horizontally. We can't find life, love, rest, identity, security, purpose, or deep inner peace in creation, only in the Creator.

I've already talked about some of the ways social media can work for us. But it also produces so much anxiety by way of comparison. The problem with comparison is that it encourages us to follow other people's vision for our life instead of the One who made our life's vision. Why would we want to do that?

The cure for comparison is contentment. As Paul tells the young preacher Timothy, "godliness with contentment is great gain" (1 Tim. 6:6). Until we cultivate a heart of gratitude and contentment, the peace we pursue will inevitably elude us. Without gratefulness, we are prone to hardness of heart and darkness of mind. All pain. No gain. But don't panic! There's hope for peace when we trust in Jesus Christ, the greatest gain.

We don't just want to know *about* God's peace but never truly experience God' peace.

Trusting, Not Knowing

A lasting faith moves beyond the confines of reason and comparison, because peace does not come when all of our questions are answered. Peace comes only when we are living into God's perfect plan for our lives. The only question that ultimately matters is whether or not we're willing to follow Jesus.

To trust Jesus, we must spend time in Scripture, not because it will answer all of our questions but because it will make us more like Him. If you want to know God's plan for your life, that's it: be like Jesus. We must study God's Word so we can educate, encourage, and exhort one another; examine ourselves; and learn to equip others in His truth.

Believing His Word requires us to move beyond the borders of rationality. We can't trust our reason more than we trust the mystery of the reality that Jesus is risen. The Bible proclaims the mysteries of God from Genesis through the book of Revelation. Everyone in the Bible who knew God, loved God, and obeyed God had questions. Some of those people got answers while others didn't. And those of us living in the present age won't get all of our answers just by knowing the Bible back to front. Any theologian will gladly tell you that even a seminary education will not bring peace.

If you long for perfect peace, consider the following words from the prophet Isaiah:

> You keep him in perfect peace
>> whose mind is stayed on you,
>> because he trusts in you.
> Trust in the LORD forever,
>> for the LORD God is an everlasting rock. (Isa. 26:3–4
>> ESV)

This passage explains the passageway to peace. We will never experience God's peace by just *knowing* about God but only by *trusting* Him. We do this primarily by opening our hearts and admitting we need His help. We Go In. We stay our minds on Him. A prideful heart can't do this. A trusting heart can. A heart filled with pride holds it all inside. And a heart filled with pride has a lot in common with a heart filled with anxiety. My beloved friend Paul Sohn told me the other day that the average high school kid today has the same level of anxiety as that of the average psychiatric patient in the early 1950s. We have to give God our anxiety and pride because we cannot do this one on our own. If we never Go In to God, desperate in prayer and trusting His Word, we will live anxious lives. We will never live into His perfect plan. It takes faith to exchange our mess for God's best.

✚ REACH OUT

Awakening to God's Peace

Once we experience God's peace in our lives, He asks us to take that peace and share it with others. We are to be contagious

carriers of God's perfect peace to people in chaos. We write "Rest In Peace" on the headstones of the dead, but peace isn't just for the dead. Jesus came back from the dead so those living could not just rest in peace but perpetually live in it! By God's divine providence, Jesus died and came back to life to restore the peace of God to His creation. Darkness, destruction, and decay are defeated; sorrow, sickness, and suffering are now subjugated. By His sacrifice for us, Jesus has provided a peace the world can never offer—a peace we can enjoy now and forever and a peace we can show to others when we Reach Out.

But our world is in so much pain, beset constantly by grief and suffering, that not many people know about the peace of Jesus. It's our job to deliver the message. My friend AJ recently reminded me of this truth. It was an early Sunday morning, and AJ was outside our church cleaning up the wooded campus in preparation for the services that would start in a few hours. Suddenly there was a lot of screaming. I ran through the hallways. I heard someone shout that AJ had been attacked outside by a deer. I frantically searched for him, hoping he was okay. I rushed into the lobby and found him sitting in silence, catching his breath. His sweater was destroyed, torn up by the antlers of a big buck.

"AJ! Are you all right?"

"Rashawn," he said slowly, "I'm more than okay. Honestly, I'm honored."

"What? You could have been killed."

"Yeah, but I've been asking God for more strength lately. Today God answered my prayer."

I sat there, stunned at AJ's trust in Jesus. This was a scary situation, but AJ had peace because he trusted in the Prince of Peace. Nobody would have been surprised if AJ freaked out. But he didn't. Instead, he spent the morning at church, even though he was roughed up, reaching out to thousands of people and giving witness to the One who provides a peace that goes beyond all understanding.

Jesus is our one and only hope for peace in a chaotic world. He not only brings us peace but is our peace. This world is scary, but if you place your trust in Jesus, you can not only have peace but bring peace into each and every situation you find yourself in.

TAKING THE NEXT STEP

PAUSE AND PONDER

Jesus doesn't only bring us peace but is our peace.

PRESS INTO PRAYER

There is so much we will never know.
So many questions that go unanswered.
But there is also so much we do know.
We know . . .

We are worthy.
We are precious.
God paid a high price for us.
God died for us.
God believes in us.
God chose us.
God loves us.
Just the way we are.

Lord,

Thank You so much for giving me the gift of peace. May I seek it and pursue it daily. I want to know You more and engrave Your Word on my heart. May I continue to find You in the midst of chaos and in the midst of every decision I make moving forward. I want Your still, calm voice to be louder than the chaos.

PROVE TO BE A PRACTICAL PIONEER

Today, when you feel anxious, take a minute to pray before you try anything else—don't grab your phone, don't head for the fridge. Grab your Bible and sit for a few minutes in God's peace.

Conviction

Be gentle and ready to forgive; never hold grudges. Remember, the Lord forgave you, so you must forgive others.

COLOSSIANS 3:13 TLB

Jesus answered, "Very truly I tell you, no one can enter the kingdom of God unless they are born of water and the Spirit. Flesh gives birth to flesh, but the Spirit gives birth to spirit. You should not be surprised at my saying, 'You must be born again.'"

JOHN 3:5-7

COME UP

Cooler Than Cool

When you were in your mother's womb, preparing to make your grand entrance into the world, her family and friends anticipated your arrival and showered her with love. After you were born, the cameras flashed and phone calls blasted from coast to coast. The message spread that *you* had finally arrived. Flights were booked and grandparents were hooked. You were all that and a bag of chips!

Sadly, I know this isn't the case for everyone reading this right now—but wait! Here's a truth you can joyfully grasp and embrace: even if your parents and grandparents didn't celebrate your birth, God did. I love the words David shared in Psalm 27:10, "Though my father and mother forsake me, the Lord will receive me." Way back when your parents had "heart eyes" for each other and didn't even have you in mind yet, God did. Jesus was actively engaged in every waking moment of your existence. He came to give you a new spiritual birth that will radically transform you from the inside out, from who you were into who you were created to be.

The day you were born was a miracle, even if your family circumstances were messy. And no matter what's happened since then, you're still an amazing gift not only to the world but especially to God, who created you cell by cell, bone by bone, organ by organ. You are fearfully and wonderfully made. No one can ever take away your worth. There's no one else on this planet who has your smile. The FBI could search through the more than seven billion other people residing on this planet, scan all their fingerprints, and they'd never find one that matches *you*. You are *that* special.

God is a Creator, not a duplicator. There are hundreds, thousands, perhaps millions of people who need the hero God has placed inside you. You were born to awaken and free your hero from the confines of your past and walk into God's acceptance so you can leave your mark on this world for Jesus. You are supposed to be here—on this earth, in this place—for such a time as this. People you've loved deeply may have turned their backs on you, but not God. No matter who may have rejected you, you are safe in God's loving arms.

Does any of this make you uncomfortable? You're not alone if you're squirming in your seat or skimming these lines. Accepting the truth of our God-given worth is not easy—it takes conviction. And conviction is the opposite of cool. The culture of cool has utterly consumed our hearts and laid the conviction to pursue the cross on the back burner. The culture of cool is a harsh master, and its weapon is rejection. A part of me (sometimes a huge part) is afraid of rejection. Can you relate? We may be worthy in God's eyes, but when we're caught up in the culture of cool, we sure won't feel worthy. Thankfully, the culture of cool isn't the costume we're called to wear. The cross is what we are called to take up daily and put on our backs. Not all heroes wear cool capes. Mine wore a thorn crown and a cross. What about yours?

A Call to All

We're all called to conviction. The strong, the weak, the rich, the poor. All of us. In the Gospel of Luke, we hear the remarkable account of how Mary became pregnant by the Holy Spirit and gave birth to a child who would become the Savior of the world. But if the world had its way, Jesus wouldn't have survived. He had a price on His head from His very first day. If you're not familiar with the story, King Herod sent out soldiers to kill any child under the age of two in Bethlehem, the city where Jesus was born. The Scriptures had prophesied the Messiah would soon be born, and kings like to stay on their thrones. Herod was trying to destroy God's plan, but God's plans are not easily thwarted.

Imagine the fear that Joseph and Mary must have experienced during this time. The devil kept firing arrows at the newly born

Savior of the world. But even though this beautiful baby was threatened by evil, God brought reassurance. Jesus came to save all of us. The first people to worship Jesus were shepherds. It amazes me that God would give them that honor. Shepherds were not highly regarded people in the ancient world. They were second-class citizens. The weak and lowly heard the good news first. That's not to say God cared more about the poor than others. The mighty magi also came and worshiped Jesus. God wants all people to hear His good news. God calls the first and the last. God calls the outcast and the upper class.

God saves philosophers.
God saves prostitutes.
God saves hip-hop artists.
God saves worship leaders.
God saves teachers.
God saves seminary students.
God saves drug dealers.
God saves doctors.
God saves abusers.
God saves losers, winners, saints, and sinners.
God saves all who answer the call.

I know it's not hard to think of this out of order. When we hear the word *call*, we think of all the work we're going to do *for* God. But the Bible speaks more about our call as a calling *to* God. He's not a harsh taskmaster or angry boss. He's a Friend to enjoy, a Savior to savor, and a Father to fear (deeply respect).

We're all called to conviction. We didn't choose God; He chose us. While we were stuck trying to figure out God's contact number, He was already calling our names. He chose us for Himself, first for salvation through Jesus Christ. We go from slaves to being saved, from no hope to pure joy, and it's all by simply answering His call once and for all.

In Acts 2:21, Peter says, "Everyone who calls on the name of the Lord will be saved."

Not just some. Everyone. Even the people who fall deep below the world's standards.

> Consider your calling, brothers: not many of you were wise according to worldly standards, not many were powerful, not many were of noble birth. But *God chose* what is foolish in the world to shame the wise; *God chose* what is weak in the world to shame the strong; *God chose* what is low and despised in the world, even things that are not, to bring to nothing things that are, so that no human being might boast in the presence of God. (1 Cor. 1:26–29 ESV, emphasis added)

It's astonishing to imagine God's *calling* for us is to use us to demonstrate His greatness and power through all of our weaknesses and in all of our foolishness. This is actually really comforting, but it's also very convicting. Holy Spirit, we need You. Right? We can look ridiculous, weak, and unworthy in the eyes of the world as we faithfully follow the conviction of the Holy Spirit, and we will be fulfilling God's calling. Do you believe this to be true?

God's grace is reaching out indiscriminately to all who answer His call and call upon Him. You can start where you are. No matter how strong, how weak, how rich, how poor. You can be a bricklayer or a banker. A gangster or a guard. We can move forward just as we are through the power of the Holy Spirit.

The Call Continues No Matter What Happens

Do you remember how Mary discovered she was pregnant? It's kind of a wild story.

> The angel went to her and said, "Greetings, you who are highly favored! The Lord is with you. . . . You will conceive and give birth to a son, and you are to call him Jesus. He will be great and will be called the Son of the Most High. The Lord God will give him the throne of his father David, and he will reign over Jacob's descendants forever; his kingdom will never end." (Luke 1:28, 31–33)

Crazy, right? Can you even imagine what must have been going through Mary's heart and mind? Getting pregnant before marriage in those days meant she could have been exiled from the community or even stoned to death. This was one huge task God was asking Mary to do.

Mary was confused, and she asked Gabriel how this could be true because she was a virgin.

> [Gabriel] answered, "The Holy Spirit will come on you, and the power of the Most High will overshadow you. So the holy one to be born will be called the Son of God. Even Elizabeth your relative is going to have a child in her old age, and she who was said to be unable to conceive is in her sixth month. For no word from God will ever fail." (vv. 35–37)

Nothing is impossible for God. Not even a virgin birth! By the grace of God and the power of the Holy Spirit, Mary gave birth to the true miracle baby who would eventually turn the world upside down. He would turn the harshness of hate into radical love, the dangers of darkness into glorious light, and the destiny of death into everlasting life. No one could thwart God's plan. But wait—it gets even better. This is the plan God has for your life too. He wants to give you a new birth by the same Holy Spirit who allowed Mary to give birth to Jesus. This birth will bring you a new life, one where nothing is impossible and you can be totally transformed.

He wants to give you new eyes, eyes that see His vision for the kingdom that originated from the beginning of time, long before your mother ever knew you would be in her womb. He longs to erase your self-centered plans and the influence of people who live contrary to His purposes for your life. Every step you take toward living life transformed is overshadowed by His holy, loving presence, just as Mary was overshadowed so long ago.

When you live in and from the presence of God, transformed by the Holy Spirit, change can't help but occur in your life and in the lives around you. The fruit that springs forth inside of you will also grow all around you. This can happen no matter where you are today or how far you think you are from God.

It doesn't matter how much you struggle with sin.

It doesn't matter how disloyal you were to a friend.

It doesn't matter how old or young you are.

It doesn't matter how rich or poor you are.

It doesn't matter how much better or worse you are than any other person.

By the power of the Holy Spirit, He's calling you.

The call God makes on our lives is not an easy one. In fact, the gospel calls us to die. This is a call to die to your life. A call to die to your family. A call to die to your friends. A call to die to your self-centered dreams. But this call to death is actually a call to life. Remember, Jesus came to bring us life. A life in Jesus is a life filled with the Holy Spirit, and it leads to not only life now but also life eternal. We are called to enter into death with Christ so we might rise once more in the power of Christ.

You might think God would call in a loud voice, but God's voice is gentle. That's why the psalmist says we must "be still" to know God is God (Ps. 46:10). One day, God instructed the prophet Elijah to go stand on a mountain because He Himself was about to pass by. The Bible then says a powerful wind tore the mountains apart and shattered the rocks, but the Lord was not in the wind. After the wind an earthquake erupted, but the Lord was not in the earthquake. After the earthquake came a fire, but the Lord was not in the fire. After the fire came—you guessed it—a *gentle whisper*. And it was in the whisper that God was found (1 Kings 19:10–13).

God rarely shouts. He gently whispers a fresh wind into the hearts of the lifeless. The voices of this world roar for our attention, but the gentle giant of the Holy Spirit draws us into solitude to peacefully hear God in our hearts: *You are My child, and I have plans for you. These plans aren't to harm you but to prosper you and give you hope and a future* (Jer. 29:11). These are words we all need to hear, but we can't if we allow the screams of the world to constantly bombard us. We have to cancel out the noise if we want to know that God is who God says He is. He doesn't shout above the noise; He simply asks that we turn it down and turn Him up. We have to turn down our need to be cool and turn up our desire to be convicted. His voice is there for us to hear. The only question is whether or not we're listening.

The Most Important Person on the Planet

The most important person on the planet isn't Donald Trump. Sorry, Republicans. But it's not Barack Obama or Bernie Sanders either. Sorry, Democrats. The most important person on the planet isn't LeBron James or Drake or Taylor Swift. The most important person on the planet isn't your pastor or your lawyer or even your favorite Instagram influencer. The most important Person on the planet is the Holy Spirit.

God sent the Holy Spirit to finish the work He started in the book of Genesis, the most important work in the world. In the Old Testament we primarily see the work of God the Father. In the New Testament we primarily see the work of God the Son, Jesus. And today we primarily see the work of the Holy Spirit, the third Person of the Trinity, whom Jesus introduced like this:

> When He, the Spirit of truth, has come, He will *guide you into all truth*; for He will not speak on His own authority, but whatever He hears He will speak; and He will tell you things to come. He will glorify Me, for He will take of what is Mine and declare it to you. All things that the Father has are Mine. Therefore I said that He will take of Mine and declare it to you. (John 16:13–15 NKJV, emphasis added)

Jesus poured out His Spirit onto us. We can hear from the most important Person on the planet if we'll be quiet enough to hear His voice. The One with the most wisdom will not only return our phone call but is calling out to us. I don't know about you, but none of the so-called important people on this planet are calling me about anything! Don't take this for granted. God desperately wants to talk to you. All you have to do is quiet down and listen.

Conviction Is Greater Than Cool

I used to fear listening to the Holy Spirit because I thought I'd hear judgment. And I felt like I knew a lot about my sins already. While the Holy Spirit does convict us of sin, that is not all the Spirit does. After all, being a Christian isn't about guilt but grace. The Holy Spirit also cultivates sweet communion with God that helps us hear God's voice.

When Jesus promises to send the Holy Spirit to His followers after His death, He tells them He'll send a *paraclete.* In the ancient world, a *paraclete* was a person who came alongside another during a time of legal difficulty to advocate for them. Though He is not physically present with us, Jesus sent the Holy Spirit to advocate for us. This means the Holy Spirit doesn't convict us simply to make us feel guilty but to help us follow after Jesus. If we are already walking that way, the Spirit will allow us to rejoice. If we aren't, the Spirit will convict and guide us back into a closer walk. Conviction, then, isn't something to fear but celebrate. That's much better than ignoring the Holy Spirit, because the Bible says one day we'll stand before the Lord and be held to account for our lives. It would be better to take the help from our paraclete now!

That said, many of us struggle to follow the Holy Spirit's conviction instead of the desire to be cool. Billy Graham, one of the greatest preachers of all time, knew something about conviction. But he also felt that pull to be cool in the sight of the world. Here's what he had to say about it: "Be attractive and winsome, but do not compromise your convictions for the sake of popularity."[1]

Here's a little secret I discovered that helps me: *conviction* makes your influence look *credible* while *cool* makes your influence look *cheap.*

What's the difference between cool and convicted? I'll spell it out. Cool is doing what's fun. Cool follows the warm and fuzzy feelings. Cool seeks the momentary over the permanent. Cool is relative but restrictive. Cool conforms to the norm.

Conviction never compromises the truth for trends. Conviction cultivates Christlikeness. Conviction, unlike cool, doesn't change. Conviction is willing to speak truth into situations where it would otherwise be easier to stay silent.

If you want to be cool, you'll do anything for acceptance. "Cool" cannot guide the heart of a Christian. If we base our daily decisions on being cool, we will trash the teachings of Christ. Jesus told us to not be surprised when the world hates us, because it first hated Him (John 15:18). Christianity is not a formula for popularity but a path to supernatural transformation through conviction. Unlike cool, conviction points to the truth, and the truth always points to the cross.

We abandon our right to be cool when we choose the conviction of Jesus's cross. At times, carrying the convictions of the cross will be extraordinarily difficult. Don't forget: we have the Holy Spirit to advocate for us at every step!

⮕ GO IN

Obsessed with Acceptance

I used to serve a large church in South Dakota. It's hard to admit, but I was an obsessive people pleaser who hated confrontation. I never shared my opinion and I smiled all the time. When given the opportunity to provide feedback, I'd be encouraging but withhold any words of challenge. I cared too much about the opinions of others to be honest with them. But then God spoke a word to me. He knew I couldn't stay where I was. I came up to Him with nothing but my desire to be cool, and He told me it was time to Go In. One day, while I was driving to a family reunion, God said, *Rashawn, on your quest to be cool you've been trashing your actual eternal virtues, which are faith, hope, and love.* Ouch.

When I wasn't concerned about cool, I had faith that God keeps His promises. I had hope that Jesus would return soon. And I had love overflowing for God, for myself, and for my neighbors. Cool had taken all of that away.

I clenched the steering wheel, smiled, and said, "Thank You, Lord!"

Then God said, *Son, you don't have to fear anyone. Put your trust in Me. After all, don't you remember what love is?* I recalled my Scripture devotional from that week and said aloud, "Perfect love casts out fear" (1 John 4:18 ESV). Moments later, God reminded me what the Bible says about love—or rather *doesn't say.* First Corinthians 13 doesn't say "love is nice." It says love "rejoices with the truth" (v. 6).

The Lord continued speaking to me: *You fear rejection, Rashawn. Don't focus on being cool; focus on the conviction I put in you to love Me and My people.*

I spent the rest of that drive in prayer, listening to the Holy Spirit minister to me about my toxic need for acceptance, approval, and applause. I'd traded my genuine conviction to serve Jesus for the fragile feeling of being cool. God showed me that it was impossible to honestly love people if I wasn't willing to *be* honest with people. A person who loves God will speak truth in all situations for the sake of other people.

The truth doesn't really matter to someone cool. Looking cool is all they want. Watch the cool guy on any college football team and you'll see what I mean. He doesn't care about taking instruction or building other players up. He isn't thankful for the eight touchdowns he got last season. He doesn't want anything to do with the team tutor. He just wants to look cool. He is demanding, argumentative, and rebellious because the only thing that matters to him is *him*.

The irony of being cool is that it's *not* cool. It's actually miserable to be around. People who obsess over themselves drive others away because they live according to their own thoughts as opposed to the thoughts of God. Only when selfishness becomes insignificant and selflessness becomes significant will God's glory shine in someone's life.

Take a look in the mirror. Do you see God's glory shining through you? He called you to stand firm in your Christlike conviction and not compromise His loving sacrifice for the sake of your coolness. Cool is the way of culture. Conviction is the way of Christ.

Conviction Overpowers Fear

Bob Goff says that "fear calls out our doubts; God calls out our names."[2] The gentle voice that whispers in the dark does not incite fear but gives us the courage to overcome fear. I once heard a story about a Chinese mother who showed tremendous courage in the face of fear. She had Gone In to God in prayer—in this case, literally. She had been spreading the gospel of Jesus. When the Chinese government found out, they locked her up in jail along with her five-year-old daughter, because there was no other person to care for the child. The other prisoners and even the prison guards hated the mother for this. They didn't understand why she would force herself and her daughter to suffer when all she had to do was renounce her faith in order to be free. The prison warden said, "Don't you have concern for your daughter? Reject Jesus and we'll let you both go free."

Doubt crept in. *Leaving would be good for my daughter*, she thought. *It's wrong of me to make her suffer like this.* "Okay," the mother said to the warden. "We want to be released." The warden then made the woman stand on a stage before twenty thousand people and renounce her faith. She did it, and they were immediately freed.

Walking home, the young daughter spoke up. "Mommy, today Jesus was heartbroken by your words."

The mother said, "But you were sad in prison. I had to get you out of that place."

Her daughter replied, "We should go back to jail for Jesus. I promise I won't cry again."

They turned around and went back to the prison. The mother asked for the warden and said, "You told me I should lie about my faith for my daughter's sake. Thankfully, she had more courage to share the goodness of my Savior than I did." They both were shackled and placed back in a cold cell at the bottom of the prison. But the courageous daughter no longer cried. Instead, she rejoiced because they were no longer afraid of anything. They may not have been set free from their chains, but love struck away the chains of fear from their souls. This is what God's love does. It wipes away our fears.

The truth is we have nothing to fear because of God's love, a love that will never change or fade. It is a love that no one can take away. A love from which we need no other person's acceptance. A love we receive not through being cool but convicted. A love that gently whispers, *You are enough.*

⊕ REACH OUT

When the World Lets You Down

Nothing's cooler than getting our own way. That means our conviction can show up in a big way when we're disappointed. I had a long conversation about this with my mentor, Shawn Maguire. He's a therapist and an incredible man of God. The irony of his name being Shawn and mine Rashawn is not lost on us. I'm like the "ra-peat"—newer and better—Shawn.

I asked Shawn how I should respond when other people attack me with negativity. He said, "We have to set the tone. When the odds are against us, we must be confident that God is *for* us."

I asked him what he thought that would look like, and we had a great discussion. We came away with some rules to help set the tone and come across as convicted rather than cool. These rules can help us all Reach Out to a world in conflict.

Rule 1: Fighting < Forgiveness

Give up. This allows you to heal yourself and your enemies. Abraham Lincoln once gave a speech at the height of the Civil War in which he described the Confederates as fellow human beings who were simply in error. Afterward, he was harshly criticized for describing them so generously. One woman suggested he should have described the Southerners as enemies who must be destroyed, to which Lincoln replied, "Why, madam, do I not destroy my enemies when I make them my friends?"[3] Now that's an example of the transforming power of Jesus's command to love our enemies. A spirit of forgiveness not only sets us free but also vanquishes the enemy. We must stay gentle in a world where everyone is at war.

Rule 2: Emotions < Devotion

It's better to be led by God's Spirit than our emotions. The level of our devotion to God will determine the amount of temptation we can withstand. Little prayer, little power. Lots of prayer, lots of power. Talk to any mental health professional, and they'll tell you that while our emotions are important, they can also lie to us. Emotions are not always good indicators of reality. It's important to be in touch with our emotions, but following Jesus will not always feel like the thing we'll want to do the most. That's when we must trust the Spirit to guide us no matter how we are feeling.

Jesus fought the same frigid winds of distraction, doubt, and discouragement that we feel, but they never kept Him from trusting in God's unwavering love. Jesus longs to help us trade the flimsy blankets of our emotions for His Spirit-filled devotion. Even Mother Teresa, famous for her work with the poor, confessed that she went for years without feeling the presence of God. She was more committed to devotion than emotion.[4]

Rule 3: Happiness < Holiness

We are not called to a happy life but a holy life. When we are holy, we will become happy. In Romans 8:28–30 we get to see that before we existed, God knew us and set us apart for His purpose. When we embrace this we not only become happy but also receive fulfillment and joy in living a life of purpose. Blaise Pascal said, "There is a God-shaped vacuum in the heart of each man which cannot be satisfied by any created thing but only by God the Creator, made known through Jesus Christ."[5] Jim Carrey put it this way: "I think everybody should get rich and famous and do everything they ever dreamed of so they can see that it's not the answer."[6]

Rule 4: Reaction < Reflection

Respond to the Holy Spirit *before* reacting to people. Immature people react. Wise people respond. What's the difference? Reaction is immediate. Responding requires taking a moment to consult the Holy Spirit. My friend Ryan Casey Waller studied under the great spiritual writer Dallas Willard, and he said Dallas never responded to anything without taking a long moment of silence. Sometimes it was awkward, but Dallas didn't care because he understood how important this was. He didn't react to anything. He only responded. Ryan says Dallas was the gentlest person he ever met.

Rule 5: Lashing Out < Leaning In

Yield to the Holy Spirit before you yell at a person. Righteous anger is definitely a thing. After all, Jesus overturned tables in the temple when He saw what the religious leaders had done to His Father's house of prayer. That said, lashing out in anger is not usually the best response. The Bible calls us to turn the other cheek and to respond to hate with love. Most of the time that means we should lean in to whoever is offending us to offer them love and respect as opposed to lashing out. When this gets hard and we want to take justice into our own hands, we should remember the Lord says that vengeance is His (Rom. 12:19). One day He will make things right. Until then, we should love and leave justice to the Judge.

Rule 6: Selfishness < Submission

Writing to the Galatians, Paul said, "I have been crucified with Christ and I no longer live, but Christ lives in me. The life I now live in the body, I live by faith in the Son of God, who loved me and gave himself for me" (2:20). In Christ we die to ourselves in order to find true freedom. This pattern can even be seen in the Old Testament. God frees His people from slavery in Egypt, but the climax of that story is not the crossing of the Red Sea when their enemies are destroyed by the crashing water behind them. The real climax is when Moses returns from Mount Sinai with the Ten Commandments. You see, God didn't free His people so they could simply be free. He freed them so they were no longer submissive to Pharaoh but could become submissive to God. In that kind of submission, obeying God's commands, we find genuine freedom.

Rule 7: Me, Myself, and I < Mission

As Christians we are called to be one body in Christ. This means we are all connected in ways that cannot be undone. As Paul writes in his first letter to the Corinthians:

> Our bodies have many parts. . . . So it is with the "body" of Christ. Each of us is a part of the one body of Christ. Some of us are Jews, some are Gentiles, some are slaves, and some are free. But the Holy Spirit has fitted us all together into one body. We have been baptized into Christ's body by the one Spirit, and have all been given that same Holy Spirit.
> Yes, the body has many parts, not just one part. (1 Cor. 12:12–14 TLB)

Consequently, we are called to always care more about the whole than our individual selves. The body is always greater than the sum of its parts. Keeping the mission of the church primary helps all of us understand our subservient role. None of us is more important than the overall mission of advancing the gospel, as Paul writes in Philippians. The reality is that we are all going to drop the ball at some point. We're going to disappoint one another. When we do, we must be gentle with one another as we're told in Galatians 6:1, remembering that we're all a part of the same body. One member of the body must not attack another member when in pain but rather help restore. Reacting harshly never edifies the body. It only terrifies. Instead, we respond gently as the Holy Spirit responds gently to us. It's only when we love like Jesus that we experience true evidence of God's power working in our lives. Bob Goff said it best: "The way we love the people we don't agree with is the best evidence that the tomb is empty."[7]

A good therapist offers good answers.

A profound philosopher offers brilliant ideas.

A professional psychologist offers a confident diagnosis.

A wise counselor offers awesome advice.

Only Jesus Christ, crucified, risen, and ascended, made a way for God's Spirit to truthfully liberate our souls to love even when people let us down.

TAKING THE NEXT STEP

PAUSE AND PONDER

Conviction will always make your influence look credible; cool makes your influence look cheap.

PRESS INTO PRAYER

Jesus fed 5,000,
but only 500 followed Him after lunch was served.
He had 12 disciples,
but only 3 went farther in the Garden,
and sadly only 1 stood with Him at the cross.
Well, 2 if you count His mama.
The closer you get to the cross, the stronger your conviction grows, the smaller the crowd becomes.

Lord,

Thank You for being my comfort during hard times. When it's hard for me to walk in conviction and easy for me to compromise, I'm reminded that You've given me Your Holy Spirit, and I can do all things through Christ who gives me strength. May I give up my need to be seen as cool for Your gift of conviction and find joy in pleasing You over pleasing people.

PROVE TO BE A PRACTICAL PIONEER

What are some areas in your life in which you may be compromising your love for Christ for the approval of the crowds?

START with COOL, END with CONVICTION

5

Faithfulness

If we are faithless, he remains faithful—
for he cannot deny himself.

2 TIMOTHY 2:13 ESV

We can trust God's heart even when we can't trace His path.

GREG LAURIE

⬆ COME UP

Diamond in the Sky

The diamond in the sky doesn't lie. The words of my Army sergeant clanged around in my head as I headed out into the woods to begin my land navigation test. The sun was shining bright, and the path before me was clear. The challenge to complete the intensive course was real. Game on.

Making it to Point One on the course was relatively easy. Point Two . . . not so much. Point Three was a different story entirely. By then the sun had dropped in the sky and darkness was spreading across the horizon. My nerves were on edge. According to my little pocket map, Point Four was buried somewhere far deeper in the woods of Washington State.

As the dark settled in around me, fear took hold of my soul. I couldn't recognize my surroundings, and my hope of finishing the course was fading faster than the waning daylight. Then I realized I'd lost my map. My anxiety took over. I didn't know which direction I just came from and which direction I needed to walk next.

No book bag.

No Apple watch.

No map.

No compass.

No flashlight.

Certainly, no iPhone in hand. No Twitter when you're busy trying not to be something's dinner. Seriously! With a heart full of despair I simply hoped God wouldn't ignore my silent prayer for help.

How can I survive without a terrain map or a navigation tool? The next ten minutes felt like ten years. North looked like south, and west looked a whole lot like east. Desperate for direction, I stopped in my tracks. I couldn't rely on marks on a paper, but I could remember the remarks of my sergeant.

The diamond in the sky doesn't lie.

It clicked in my brain.

We all have moments of realization, moments when simple things in life become so clear that we stop and dwell on the clarity. For many, the moment comes and goes. For others, it creates an unexpected fork in the road.

Could that "diamond in the sky" be the North Star?

The North Star has shone brightly from generation to generation, serving as a guide for everyone from ancient nomads to Cub Scout dads. We follow it because we can trust it. The light of the crescent moon is beautiful, but I would never follow it. I've enjoyed countless shooting stars, with the awe and wonder of that breathtaking streak across the horizon. But as beautiful as a shooting star is, it would prove fatal to put your trust in it for direction. The North Star, however, stays true. I followed that star through the woods all night in my course, and it took me to Point Four. Like the North Star, God's faithfulness never fades. The good news is that God is a better guide than even the North Star, because God can guide us not only physically but spiritually.

We can trust that even in the twists and turns of life, God's in control, and He's forever faithful. That's what faith is all about. Our current situation may be uncertain. Our future may be unknown. Our career may be unpredictable. Our relationships may be undefined. But there is one thing that will always remain certain and true in our life: God's faithfulness. He loves us, He will lead us, and He will take care of us. In every season He will remain the same loving Father who walks with us every step of the way. We have nothing to be afraid of when we face every moment with Him.

Fully Faithful

God is the most excellent example of faithfulness; He will never break a promise to His children (Num. 23:19). You are His child. He loves you like crazy! Yes, you!

Allow your heart to know His love is true, truer than the North Star. He's made it possible for you to enjoy His presence right now, fully. What happens when friends and family fail you? When you need them but they don't show up? God never leaves you, and He never fails you. He will always be there for you.

The only reason it's possible for us to have faith in God is because God was first faithful to us. Faithfulness is at the very core of God's character.

You may not be able to trust the words of people; you may not even be able to trust your own thoughts. But you can surely believe God and His Word. You may be resting on or wrestling with the promise that God is faithful. Either way, no matter how you feel, it's true. He is faithful. Timothy was confidently reminded by his friend Paul, "If we are faithless, [God] remains faithful" (2 Tim. 2:13). This is important, because being able to trust in Jesus fully is the beginning of abundant life. We must fully trust in Jesus to be full of faith. As our faith increases, our faithfulness to God will grow. We live by faith, not by sight (2 Cor. 5:7). Faith is not a human act; it's an act of God's Spirit stirring in us, drawing us closer to Himself.

I understand this might be hard to accept. It is for me. Sometimes I don't know where to start with faith. Just start where you are! For real—stop searching and start stepping.

Faith can feel like a heavy burden we're responsible for carrying on our own. But the truth is God wants to foster it in us and carry it for us. In Matthew 11:28–30, Jesus said,

Come to me, all you who are weary and burdened, and I will give you rest. Take my yoke upon you and learn from me, for I am gentle and humble in heart, and you will find rest for your souls. For my yoke is easy and my burden is light.

This is not an empty promise. The right direction isn't to step back toward your past habits nor toward the people around you, but rather toward Jesus. If we'll move toward Jesus, He'll give us rest. He'll give us the faith we need to carry on by taking our burdens upon Himself.

Woven throughout the Scriptures are stories of ordinary men and women who believed in the extraordinary God, the true diamond in the sky who cannot lie. They were faithful to Him, regardless of what they had seen, heard, or even felt; irrespective of who was with them; and despite who was against them. No matter how awful or awesome the circumstances, they trusted God and experienced His faithfulness.

Abel offered a pure sacrifice by faith and was commended as righteous by God.

Enoch's faith pleased God so much he never experienced death.

Noah obeyed God's command to build the ark and spared his family from the floods.

Abraham obeyed God and left his land for a new land where God made his "descendants as numerous as the stars in the sky" (Gen. 22:17).

Jacob's faith was rewarded when God gave him a son named Joseph who would save millions of people, both Israelites and Egyptians.

Moses led the people of Israel out of slavery and into freedom.

Rahab, a prostitute, welcomed God's spies, saving her family from the fall of Jericho.

I could go on for pages. The point is that all of these people were quite ordinary but did extraordinary things because they trusted God's faithfulness and allowed Him to work marvelous wonders in their lives. God's faithfulness calls us out of the ordinary and toward the extraordinary.

Before We Are Ready

I attended over a dozen different schools before graduating because my father was in the military. I hated the pressure of having to make new friends every August. As a grown man, I struggle with seeking the approval of others instead of resting in God's acceptance. During my first year working as a prison guard, I was assigned to watch over a high-profile inmate. This man had committed horrific crimes that were very public in nature. Since I was his guard, I was an instant target of his enemies in the jail. These inmates insulted me nonstop, calling me names and threatening violence. For a guy who likes to be liked, it was awful. I was reliving the worst moments from my childhood all day, every day.

One day a really rough dude named Straight Laced started walking toward me. As he did, the other inmates began to scatter. *Not good*, I thought. I steadied myself for a fight. But when he got close he smiled wide. He hadn't come to fight me but to befriend me. At that moment my heart broke because I realized I hated the men who had rejected me. I assumed Straight Laced wanted to do me harm, but that wasn't the case at all. We became good friends, and his smile brightened up that jail for me on many of the darker days.

Straight Laced came for me like Jesus comes for us all: before we are ready. I didn't deserve to have Straight Laced as my friend. I had hatred in my heart toward him and any other inmates like him. But he made the first move. God doesn't wait for us to befriend Him. Instead, He befriends us. He does this even with His enemies, as we learn in Romans 5:8, when Paul says, "But God demonstrates his own love for us in this: While we were still sinners, Christ died for us." God doesn't ask us to make the friend request, merely to accept His.

There is no surer path to sadness than rejecting friendship with Jesus. If we don't allow Jesus to befriend us, then we don't get to experience His faithfulness. Think about it this way. We have to earn most of our relationships, right? We have to do something or perform in some way to attract people. But Jesus offers friendship with no prerequisites. We don't have to be funny or successful to make Him want to spend time with us. He just wants to spend time with us! Jesus didn't look you up on eHarmony or Christian Mingle to see if you shared His interests and desires. He bases His friendships solely on who He is: Love. We will never be nice enough, smart enough, rich enough, or great enough to deserve a friend like Jesus.

If you're anything like me, sin makes you feel unworthy of friendship. I think, *If anyone really knew who I am or what I have done, nobody would want to be friends with me.* Have you ever felt that way? If so, I have news for you: Jesus wants to be your friend. The Bible repeatedly tells us that Jesus is a friend to the sinner, and He came not to save those who have it all together but those of us who are sick and knee-deep in sin. Jesus went so far as to say that He didn't even want to call us servants but friends instead. This is the greatest person who ever lived calling us His friends.

Good Friends Are Good Guides

You need good friends when life gets hard. A listening ear and wise counsel are welcome in adversity. But even the best friends are limited in their ability to guide us because they—like us—can be led astray by their own hearts. God's heart, however, is perfect, and His counsel will never lead us astray.

God promises to stick closer than a brother. He also has full knowledge of the condition of our hearts. He protects us from ourselves when our hearts are sick. "For out of the heart come evil thoughts—murder, adultery, sexual immorality, theft, false testimony, [and] slander" (Matt. 15:19). The prophet Jeremiah said, "The heart is deceitful above all things, and desperately sick; who can understand it?" (Jer. 17:9 ESV). The truth is that we often return endlessly to our own sin and remain in our brokenness. But the promise of the Lord is that He'll be our faithful friend, trustworthy and always reliable. He'll send us in the best direction.

I know some people find it awkward to imagine having a relationship with a God they cannot see. I get that. But the thing I struggle with even more is my unworthiness. Why would a perfect God have any dealings with me, a fragile and sinful man? It blows my mind that the Creator of the universe longs to be my friend. But it's true. I once heard my good friend Greg Laurie speak wisdom that squarely addressed my doubts. He said, "God doesn't grade on a curve; He grades on the cross." Yes! No religion. No rituals. No church services or ceremonials. It is Christ's work alone. The sacrifice of Jesus on the cross restored our relationship with God. Our friendship with God is only possible because of the grace of God. "So now we can rejoice in our wonderful new relationship with God because our Lord Jesus Christ has made us friends of God" (Rom. 5:11 NLT).

Every day I'm working to grasp the sobering truth of God's love for me. I don't just want to be God's friend; I want God to be my best friend. I long to share *all* my experiences with Him, not just the good stuff. I want this because I know He can handle it and also because our relationship, like any genuine friendship, requires reciprocity. To sustain a friendship, two people must have constant conversation, display vulnerability, and engage in accountability. It can't be one-sided. Both must talk and listen in ways that are often uncomfortable. It's the same with Jesus. If we really want to be best friends, we have to open ourselves up to Him. This can be scary, but remember His faithfulness. Start with remembering who He is. Emmanuel. God *with* us. He will be infinitely faithful to us even when our own faith wanes.

⊕ REACH OUT

To Live Is Christ

Before Paul became a follower of Jesus, he was a religious Pharisee. He knew everything there was to know about Jewish law. In his religion, he was the best of the best. He came from the right family, he had the right education, and he lived the right kind of life. And so when other Jews claimed that Jesus, a nobody from nowhere, was the long-awaited Messiah of the Jewish people, Paul began to persecute them with every ounce of his religious zeal. He had good intentions—he believed he was doing right by God. There was only one problem.

He was wrong.

Paul was on his way to Damascus to round up some more Christians when the resurrected Jesus appeared to him and said, "Why are you persecuting me?" (Acts 9:4). In this moment Paul not only understood Jesus was the Messiah but that Jesus also wanted a deep friendship with Paul despite his mess. He was literally blinded by the experience for three days. But his heart could finally see the truth!

Paul's entire life changed. Instead of persecuting Christians he began to boldly proclaim that he now considered everything else as rubbish in comparison to having a friendship with Christ. Everything: His pedigree. His education. His authority. Paul saw his whole life for what it was when compared with Jesus's friendship: trash (Phil. 3:4–9).

Paul understood this world cannot satisfy our souls. Only God can do that. Everything dims in comparison to knowing Christ. Even if we gain everything this world has to offer, if we don't have Christ, we don't have anything.

> Meeting him in his mess,
> loving him through it, and leading him out of it.
> The hate-filled enemy became a love-filled friend of
> Jesus.
> He became a friend who was faithful to the end.

Our unadulterated friendship with God is crucial for bringing others into friendship with Him. If we want to make people faithful friends in God, our lives must look as if Jesus, and not possessions, is our peak prize.

We use money to show that God, not possessions, is our treasure. The moment we decide to place our hope in the safety net of this world, we allow hopelessness to become our spiritual monument.

Embrace the mess; that's where the growth is. Your mess is where your outreach begins. If it wasn't messy from day one, I truly don't know what Paul would've written about. It's the mess that oftentimes helps us discover, define, and deliver the message we were made to share. That message is none other than the Messiah. We are all guilty of being that dirty roommate named Paul; we, similar to Adam and Eve, also left a mess behind in the world. The Messiah is the only One who can clean it up.

What You Were Made For

We know that our mess is, well, a mess. We know there's something wrong with where we start. Why? Because we were all made for something better. God made us to live in His presence and partner with Him in caring for His creation. Just as a fish needs water and the seed needs soil, we need the presence of God. Apart from God we cannot live.

The word *eden* is Hebrew for "presence." The Garden of Eden wasn't just a physical place but an environment of God's presence. Before God made fish, He made the water. Before God made plants, He made the earth. Before God made humanity, He made Eden. In other words, He made the environment before He made what would live in the environment. He made Eden for Adam and Eve. Take a fish out of the water and it dies within minutes. Take a plant out of the soil, same thing. If you take people out of Eden (God's presence) we too will be unable to live. God created us to live in His presence, to be surrounded by His faithfulness. It can be confusing to know what it means to become the person God has made us to be. But all it really means is opening ourselves up to God's presence. We can be like Jacob when he awoke and said, "GOD is in this place—truly. And I didn't even know it!" (Gen. 28:16 MSG). He then anoints the stone pillow where he slept and calls the place *Bethel*, meaning "the house of God [and] the gate of heaven" (vv. 17–19). Now aware of God's presence, Jacob is empowered to take God's presence with him everywhere and at all times!

We reach out in faithfulness by taking God with us. We too can be like Jacob, carrying God's presence with us and partnering with God to do His work here on earth—working out our salvation, as Paul puts it in Philippians 2:12. Notice that Paul doesn't

START with DOUBT, END with FAITHFULNESS

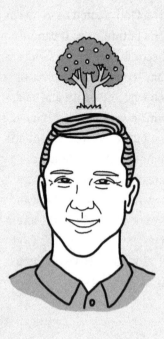

say to work *for* our salvation. He says to work *out*. This means God doesn't call us to *do* but simply to *be*. There's an enormous difference between the two. To work for something means to earn it. We don't earn salvation. Jesus has already finished the work. God offers us salvation in Him. We work out our salvation by connecting with Christ, who has already given it to us. In making us like Christ, God molds us into who He longs for us to become so we can further be empowered to do His work. I want God to work in me. The six words I long to hear when I die and cross over into eternity are, "Well done, good and faithful servant."

Keep in mind: we'll be known for our good works, but we'll be remembered by the way we allowed God to express His love through us to a hurting world. Only in doing this will we be remembered as a faithful friend.

TAKING THE NEXT STEP

PAUSE AND PONDER

Even when I'm faithless, God is faithful. When my mess is too large and my good works are too small, God remains faithful.

PRESS INTO PRAYER

Jesus doesn't look at our degrees. It's our heart He sees.
Jesus doesn't look at our popularity. He looks at our sincerity.
Jesus doesn't look at our skin color. It's our hidden sin He longs to uncover.

Jesus doesn't look at our bank account. He's looking to
deposit a greater amount in our love account.
Jesus doesn't bash us with the crimes we committed.
He's pouring out His grace, asking us to repent and
joyfully turn to Him to receive His forgiveness.
No matter where we are in life, God has more in store.

Lord,

You are faithful. Thank You for walking me through every season of my life. You have protected me from so much mess that I couldn't even see. You broke my heart for what breaks Yours, and You gladly healed so many broken areas of my life. May I continue to grow in faithfulness and be used faithfully for Your glory in all that I do. Your kingdom come, Your will be done.

PROVE TO BE A PRACTICAL PIONEER

Find ways not only to delight in the faithfulness of the gospel and God but to be a conduit and expression of God's faithfulness in your home, workplace, and wherever else you go. Imagine how God can use you, if you only have faith the size of a mustard seed (Matt. 17:20).

6

Patience

I therefore, a prisoner for the Lord, urge you to walk in a manner worthy of the calling to which you have been called, with all humility and gentleness, *with patience*, bearing with one another in love.

EPHESIANS 4:1–2 ESV, EMPHASIS ADDED

Rejoice in our confident hope. Be patient in trouble, and keep on praying.

ROMANS 12:12 NLT

 COME UP

Prayer Requires Patience

My wife's sister, Ashley, used to work for the public safety department while privately leading a reckless life. For ten years she ran away from God and her family. My wife, Denisse, prayed for

Ashley to come to the Lord, but her prayers went unanswered. Denisse became so desperate she'd yell at God to intervene. She'd share the gospel with Ashley whenever she talked with her. "Chill out with the God stuff," Ashley would reply.

Denisse felt burdened to influence her sister toward a relationship with Jesus Christ. But it seemed hopeless. Then a friend spoke truth to Denisse: "I know it's hard watching your sister struggle, but Ashley won't change what she's doing because she doesn't have the power to do it. The only One who can change her is God. All you can do is pray for her and meet her where she is by becoming love. Instead of trying to change her, trust God will do His perfect work in Ashley."

It was a light bulb moment. Denisse stopped trying to change Ashley and focused instead on praying for her. And then, two years later, everything changed. As we were having a prayer session in our living room, somebody prophesied that someone in the room had been carrying a burden for the salvation of a relative. Immediately, Denisse spoke up. "That's me! Can we pray for my sister, Ashley?"

Her request surprised me because I hadn't heard Denisse say anything about Ashley in a long time. She had really taken her friend's advice to heart and spent her time praying for Ashley instead of talking about her. Denisse was such a good example to me of how a godly person truly cares for people: no gossip, just prayer. Anyway, we prayed hard that night, and several others in the room felt freedom to share that they were concerned about the salvation of their loved ones too.

A few weeks later, I was wrapping up a session of my "Scriptures and Stories" podcast when Denisse burst into the room.

"Ashley just called me!"

"No way," I said. "What did she want?"

"She's done! She's done running from God. She gives up."

My wife and I celebrated with the angels in heaven. Another daughter of the King had chosen to come home to His wide-open arms.

God answers our prayers, but He does it in His own time. He doesn't always give us the answer we want, and He almost never gives His answer on demand. Prayer always requires patience. God isn't a vending machine who gives us what we order when we order it. His ways are above us and, ultimately, unknown to us. And so we must pray and understand that, most of the time, we're going to be waiting on God.

We have no choice but to exercise patience in prayer. We must have the ability to tolerate the time between asking for what we need and the moment God answers. As Paul writes to the church in Ephesus, "I therefore, a prisoner for the Lord, urge you to walk in a manner worthy of the calling to which you have been called, with all humility and gentleness, *with patience*, bearing with one another in love" (Eph. 4:1–2 ESV, emphasis added). We must not only wait but do so in love, bearing our lives with openness and grace, not with clenched fists. Knowing that God will do His work will give us peace. God may seem slow, but He always succeeds. Trust that.

A Patient God

Have you ever wondered why God took so long to create the universe when He could have done it instantly? Instead, He spoke creation into existence in a manner that allowed it to develop over the course of time. Why? Because God Himself is patient and reveals who He is in all of His actions.

Paul encourages us to look at creation because it teaches us something about the attributes of God (Rom. 1:20). God is patient. Our galaxy did not become what it is today in a single day. The universe is still spinning on three words: "Let there be." How beautiful is it that God's words set the galaxies, planets, even the tiny leaves falling to the ground in continual motion? I see His patience wherever I turn.

Looking down into the Grand Canyon reminds me of patience.

Looking up at the Rocky Mountains reminds me of patience.

Watching drone footage of the New York City skyline reminds me of patience.

Lying beneath the dazzling stars in Colorado reminds me of patience.

Standing in an open field watching the waterfalls in Yosemite National Park reminds me of patience.

Seeing a baby go from their birthdate to the time they graduate reminds me of patience.

Tasting a glass of old wine during a dinner in Nashville reminds me of patience.

Hearing the rustling of trees amid a cool breeze in Savannah reminds me of patience.

An Oklahoma sunrise and sunset remind me of patience.

An early morning stroll on a Southern California beach reminds me of patience.

I love what Alice Walker said: "I think it ticks God off if you walk by the color purple in a field somewhere and don't notice it. People think pleasing God is all God cares about. But anyone living in the world can see it always trying to please us back."[1]

God teaches us through the very earth we walk upon. That said, slowing down long enough to notice the brilliant patience of God is tough because we're so busy. We are a microwave people serving a crock-pot God. But, as the Bible teaches, we must "Be still before the LORD, and wait patiently for him" (Ps. 37:7). Sometimes I think it'd be great if I could whip my Bible out, rub it, and make a quick wish list for God. But that's not how it works. God isn't a genie who grants our wishes! We must learn to be patient before the Lord and trust His ways and His timing. Good things come to those who wait.

Patient with His Word

The Bible doesn't just provide information. The Bible offers transformation through the inspired words of God. Within its pages lies a power not found in any other book on the planet. It saddens me that we live in a generation that places little value upon the Bible. I could write for pages about why this might be happening, but honestly, it doesn't matter why we're not reading it. What I care about is letting people know why they should.

The Bible isn't just some old book. It's alive and breathing. No book can compare to it. It might have been written in antiquity but it speaks in specificity—to our lives. This means it will always have a word for us if we'll take the time to slow down and read it, engaging our minds and hearts. Patience must be part of the process. It's like when we meet a new friend. It takes time to get to know them, right? It takes time to learn the heart of God.

We need many moments of listening and reflecting to allow our lives to be transformed. Think of the slow, intricate, and beautiful process of the butterfly emerging from the cocoon. Transformation doesn't happen overnight but rather over the course of repeated and continuous action. The longer you spend with the Bible, the more you learn about God, yourself, sin, and God's saving plan for your life. It's all there in those inspired words. Take the time to read them! A dusty Bible can do nothing to awaken your soul.

God Is Patient with You

Jesus didn't just die for the version of you that is perfect. Jesus explicitly stated that He did not come for the righteous people but for those of us who are sick and in need of a doctor (Mark 2:17). Jesus died for the version of you that cries out from the lonely trenches of your bedroom. The version of you that wakes up from that same bedroom late for school and work. The you that forgets to put on deodorant, wears wrinkly clothes, and barely makes it to church before the start of the sermon. Jesus died for the version of you that chooses worry over worship. Jesus died for the real you, not the ideal you. Never forget that.

Jesus is patient with us as we develop into the versions of ourselves He wants us to become. "The Lord is not slow in keeping his promise, as some understand slowness. Instead he is patient with you, not wanting anyone to perish, but everyone to come to repentance" (2 Pet. 3:9). I am undeserving and unqualified to do God's work. I do it not because of who I am but because of who I know God to be. He is patient with me. I trust He will continue to do His work in me and trust His power will allow me to grow into the person He has called me to be.

We are all broken by default because this world is broken. God is active through the thread of broken humanity to produce His hope in you and me. Things crash and burn. Relationships come and go. Our hair turns from black to gray. Roses die and our heroes cry. What is beautiful and fun today fades away and vanishes tomorrow. We can't find the abundant life in temporal pleasures of this life. God patiently allows every nook and cranny of creation to die and fade in our hands so we can sprint back into His arms empty-handed. Ever since the beginning, He's worked through loss to protect us and to point us to the greatest gain, which is found in the cross. When we grasp the patience of God, we can't help but deepen our devotion to a love that is given so freely.

Bad Résumés

No résumé is ever too bad for God. Not mine and not yours. Take a moment to consider the great picture of God's patience painted across the story of the Bible. God hires unlikely people to do His work. The great leaders of our faith are not the people you and I would choose if we were God. We like flawless résumés, but God looks for those with blemishes and gaps.

Noah the drunk
Abraham the liar
Isaac the daydreamer
Jacob the deceiver
Joseph the braggart

Moses the stuttering murderer

Gideon the fearful

Samson the womanizer

Rahab the prostitute

Jeremiah and Timothy the insecure young'uns

David the adulterous murderer

Elijah the fearful

Job the bankrupt and friendless

Martha the worrier

Peter the betrayer

Lazarus the dead man

All of these people were broken and failed God and those around them. But God, in His infinite patience, kept faith in each and every one of them. Throughout the Bible, God used imperfect people like us to carry out His will, to have the biggest impact, and to do the impossible. Only through Him are our ways made perfect. As it's written in 2 Samuel, "God is my strength and power, and He makes my way perfect" (22:33 NKJV). God truly does meet us in our mess, loves us through it, and then leads us out of it. He joyfully makes all the crooked lines straight again. Most people whom God chooses are shocked that He'd choose to hire someone with such a bad history.

God doesn't look for perfection, only a willingness to follow Him. "If you are willing and obedient, you will eat the good things of the land" (Isa. 1:19). People choose other people based on position, talent, wealth; God looks for soft and open hearts, people willing to follow in whatever direction He leads.

Does that describe you? Are you willing to accept a God who accepts you no matter what you've done in the past? A God who is not only patient with imperfect people but One who propels them into His purposes? If that doesn't describe you, hear me: it can. It's completely up to you. God wants to use you. The only question is whether or not you're open to it and up for it. Go In to God in prayer. He's patiently waiting to accept your bad résumé.

Recently the internet lit up with news of a very unlikely convert to Christianity. A man with an accomplished but less than holy résumé. I'm thinking, of course, of Kanye West, one of the most influential rappers of all time. By the grace of God, the man who had referred to himself as "Yeezus" now proclaims faith in Jesus. This dramatic conversion has some comparison to Saul's Damascus road conversion to Paul. Kanye went from saying, "I am God" to "Jesus is King." He shifted his mindset from making millions to making disciples. He's been transformed from the fake Yeezus to worshiping the real Jesus. And for all of that I say, Amen!

This conversion is an opportunity for all of us to be reminded of how revolutionary the mercy and grace of God are. He wants us to know that those He radically rescues can be used immediately to rescue radically. My delight at Kanye's conversion, however, was immediately dampened when I saw how critical other Christians were of Kanye's turn toward Christ. The vast amount of hate and judgment poured forth left me dumbfounded. I've heard people say, "Kanye is crazy," "Kanye is bipolar," and "Kanye has mental problems." Honestly, I think such words are insensitive, disrespectful, and wrong, personally. "This Kanye conversion thing can't be real," some believers utter, as if God can't save people with mental and moral deficits. Isn't He the God of the impossible who makes all things possible? Don't we all have a moral deficiency?

We all have our bad habits, hiccups, and hang-ups. Scripture states plainly that we are all dead in sin. That's why we all should

START with FRUSTRATION, END with PATIENCE

stand in awe of God's grace, because apart from Christ we're all guilty. "For it is by grace you have been saved through faith—and this not from yourselves; it is the gift of God—not by works, so that no one can boast" (Eph. 2:8–9).

I don't know Kanye personally. Here's what I do know: we can sit back and be skeptical all we want, but I think it's much more freeing and God-glorifying to see the amazing fruit from this conversion: the name of Jesus is being glorified. The name of Kanye's album said it all: "Jesus Is King." It crushed the airwaves and was the #1 album on Spotify for the first couple of weeks after it released. Go, Jesus! People are listening to the name of Jesus Christ being proclaimed, and God is being glorified all around the world. It doesn't matter if it's through the mouth of Kanye West or a prominent pastor as long as Jesus's name is lifted.

> Now is the time for judgment on this world; now the prince of this world will be driven out. And I, when I am lifted up from the earth, will draw all people to myself. (John 12:32)

Here's what we can't deny: as happened because of Paul's conversion, the gospel was able to be preached.

> To people who have never heard it.
> To people who never understood it.
> To people who never expected to hear it from someone
>   they admired.
> God uses the unlikely to do the unimaginable.
>
> Our God is the God of the unlikely.
> He uses unlikely people
> to do unlikely things.
> He redeems unlikely situations

to create unlikely songs for our souls to sing.
He goes to unlikely lengths for us
to give us unlikely strength to cling.

The love of Christ through the grace of God truly changes everything. As Christians we have to remain humble and understand that God uses whomever He sees fit. Sure, we may feel our résumé is "better" than Paul's or Kanye's, but that gives us no right to question God's acceptance of it.

The world watches the actions of Christians very carefully. When it sees professing believers react critically to the news that a lost soul has been saved, our entire witness for Christ is damaged. Many people feel like their past makes them unlovable and unforgivable, and so they never come to Christ because they don't believe they are worthy of His love. When Christians react negatively to a sinner who becomes a saint, we reinforce the belief that some are beyond the grace of God. And that is just unacceptable. Millions of people will never read the Bible but they will read our actions. Our actions must scream the truth of God's love: that He wants to save as many people as are willing to accept His grace. Grace stretches out to the least likely and makes them the most likely. Grace is a gift that obliterates guilt and makes the most wonderful Christmas gift look flimsy.

There is no gift greater we will ever be given than the gift
we never earned, asked for, or deserved in the first
place.
We never deserved Jesus, we deserved far worse.
What none of us could do, Jesus did in our place.
What all of us deserved, Jesus bore on our behalf.
What we could never earn, Jesus offered as a gift.

Celebrate His grace, no matter where you are.

Start there.

Salvation lies entirely in us receiving grace, not our résumés. We do not deserve it, but we have it. We cannot earn it, but it is freely given as a gift. Our mistakes don't disqualify us; God is making all things new. Jesus was patient with us; let's be patient with others too.

⊕ REACH OUT

Be Patient with Others

In Matthew 18, Peter comes to Jesus asking about forgiveness. He wants to know how many times he has to forgive other people who wrong him, and Jesus tells him he needs to do it at least 490 times, which basically means forever. Jesus goes on to tell a parable about a king settling a debt with a debtor who owes one hundred bags of gold. The guy can't pay, and so the king orders his wife and children be sold to pay the debt. The debtor falls to his knees and begs the king to be patient with him. The king takes pity on the man and immediately cancels the debt.

The parable then takes a crazy turn. The newly forgiven debtor leaves the king and immediately encounters a man who owes him a small amount of money. When this man asks for patience, the debtor chokes him and has him thrown in prison for not repaying the debt. Horrified onlookers go back to the king and report what they have seen. The king is not pleased and has the debtor come back before him. "You wicked servant!" the king declares. "I forgave you all that debt because you pleaded with me. And should not you have had mercy on your fellow servant, as I had mercy on you?" (Matt. 18:32 ESV). Then the angry king sends the man to prison until he has paid every penny.

The king is a mouthpiece for God in this parable. The king's patience didn't mean anything in the debtor's life. He used the king's kindness for his own advantage. He trampled into the throne room of mercy just to walk out more prideful than he walked in. He forgot to delight in the wondrous grace, settling instead for a short jolt of ego. Someone should have reminded him that *his ego is not his amigo.* The temporary relief of receiving patience doesn't guarantee the awesome opportunity of returning it. We all need this reminder; it's a lesson we need to continually learn in the classroom of life.

God is patient with us but also expects us to be patient with others. Jesus tells Peter to forgive 490 times because that's what God does for us. His forgiveness is unending, and ours must be too.

Consider a few of the many verses in which God exhorts us to be patient. Look them up, turn them over in your heart and mind, and commit to living out the kind of patience God so graciously shows us.

- Be patient, bearing with one another in love (Eph. 4:2).
- Help the weak and be patient with them all (1 Thess. 5:14).
- Reprove, rebuke, and exhort with complete patience (2 Tim. 4:2).
- Be patient in tribulation (Rom. 12:12).
- Patiently endure suffering (2 Cor. 1:6).
- Patiently endure evil (2 Tim. 2:24).

- Imitate those who through faith and patience inherit the promises (Heb. 6:12).
- Be still before the Lord and wait patiently for Him (Ps. 37:7).
- Be patient until the coming of the Lord (James 5:7).

Strength to Wait

[May you be] strengthened with all power, according to his glorious might, for all endurance and patience with joy. (Col. 1:11 ESV)

Recently I was feeling overwhelmed, frustrated, and discouraged. I felt off but didn't know why. Life was good! Still, I didn't feel like myself. That's when I realized my time with the Lord had been pushed to the side. Instead of investing real time with God, I was speed-dating Him. A quick hello and then off to the next thing on my list. No wonder I felt off! I wasn't putting in the time. I started getting up early to get my heart and mind fixed on Jesus. Instant peace! I'm not kidding. God never fails to meet us where we are and move us deeper into knowledge of Him and power in Him. You and I need great strength to have patience with others, with ourselves, and with our lives. The good news is that God doesn't expect us to find this strength on our own. If we are intentional about progressing in the knowledge of God's patience, His Spirit will empower us as we go.

In this life, we'll never stop waiting. We're constantly waiting on something: that new job, that new version of ourselves, that new relationship. For years, I waited to become the best athlete I could become because I assumed I'd be good enough to make the NFL. From there, all my needs would be met. How foolish of me. I didn't make it anywhere close to the NFL. Now, I'm able to acknowledge it wouldn't have solved my problems. We all do this. We wait on that next thing we're sure will make us happy, and while we do we miss the joys of being present. And before we know it, time has passed and we've missed so much. The Bible says our lives are nothing but a vapor. The worst thing we could do is take a day for granted. Waiting, waiting, waiting . . . a person who lives as if tomorrow is promised will *procrastinate* today. But the person who lives as if tomorrow isn't promised will be *productive* today.

Waiting is an opportunity to embrace the present, not a reason to wish we were somewhere else. Can you recognize the difference?

Waiting on the Promise

As I stared out the window of my hotel room overlooking the Chicago skyline, I couldn't help but be impressed by the city lights. Their shimmer seemed to me as bright as the stars above. It was late, and I should have been tired and hungry and ready for some sleep. But after a long rap show at a nightclub on the north side of Chicago, I didn't want any of that. All I wanted was some peace. I had thought the stages and spotlights would make me happy. But staring at those city lights made it clear how dark I felt on the inside. I looked beyond them to the retreating moon. Moments later it was swallowed by dark clouds, its light extinguished. *My light*, I thought, *has also been extinguished.*

I loved making music, but in the process of making it big I lost sight of God's dream for my life. I'd pushed my agenda ahead of God's timeline for my life, and I had to suffer the consequences of living a life of no peace. This happens when we don't patiently wait on the Lord to guide our lives. Peace would evade me for years, until I finally decided to stop pursuing my own dreams and instead chose to wait for the Lord to unravel His plan for my life.

We have to be patient and trust God to reveal His plans to us in His time. That said, waiting on God can be hard. So, what does it look like to wait on God well? Glad you asked! We often see waiting as passive. If you're anything like me, doing nothing is torturous. Not many of us know how to wait well. Part of our problem is that we misunderstand what it means to wait on God. It's not a time of inaction but one of sacred privileges.

As always, the Bible points us toward a right understanding of how to do this. If you look at the word *wait* in the Hebrew, you'll see its connotations have a lot to do with being spiritually active. Although God asks us to be still and know that He is God (Ps. 46:10), He also asks that we have the proper attitude, one of expectancy, which is something that cannot be done passively. God wants us to overcome our anxiety and impatience. Instead of us fretting about what will happen, He wants us to trust that He will do His good work. His plan will be brought forth into reality. Our job is to not only trust that He's working but to be excited about what He will do. This attitude allows us to go from impatient to hopeful and hungry for whatever the Lord will do next. Having hope in God's plan is all about confident expectation that the marvelous work He began will be brought to completion (Phil. 1:6).

When we hold on to God's Word with hope in the waiting room of life, He will strengthen our hearts to endure even the most restless times. The waiting room will sometimes call us out of our career or even our calling, and it will bring us back to the heart of the One who called us.

Do you hear His voice?

He's calling you back into your simple purpose of just knowing Him and loving Him.

TAKING THE NEXT STEP

PAUSE AND PONDER

Take a moment to imagine something crazy: you are a caterpillar. Though the leaves of *waiting* taste bitter, you can slightly sense change coming for the better. The horizon dimly whispers the glory of God and the good to come. You patiently wait, never really knowing what the end result will be. But yet you still wait, expectantly. Never forget: waiting on God is never a waste of time. It's simply going inward to God with a hopeful heart for His best even amid the mess.

PRESS INTO PRAYER

Lord,

I thank You for being so patient with me. I know I have my moments where I act from emotions rather than seeking wisdom from You. May I be reminded to be quick to listen, slow to speak, and slow to become angry. May I be a reflection of You in all situations, even when life is hard and things are messy.

PROVE TO BE A PRACTICAL PIONEER

In what area of my life do I need to ask for the Spirit's power to grow more patient?

7

Self-Control

Better a patient person than a warrior,
one with *self-control* than one who takes a city.

PROVERBS 16:32, EMPHASIS ADDED

Jesus was victorious not because he never flinched, talked back, or questioned, but having flinched, talked back, and questioned, he remained faithful.

BRENNAN MANNING, *THE RAGAMUFFIN GOSPEL*

COME UP

Furious Love

In the movies, Jesus is rarely portrayed as a man with passion. He usually just strolls around, kissing babies and calmly dropping wisdom bombs. He performs miracles without breaking a sweat. The reality is that Jesus wasn't always calm. One time He went to the temple and destroyed so much property that He should have been arrested. I kind of love that.

It was Passover, and Jesus had traveled to Jerusalem to worship in the temple with other faithful Jews. When He got there, He didn't like what He saw. Men were selling cattle and other animals to the worshipers who had come to make their sacrifices to God. The religious authorities were abusing their power and taxing the faithful way too much money.

Jesus went bananas.

He created a makeshift whip and sent the animals stampeding out of the place. Then He scattered the coffers of the guys collecting the money. For an encore, He took the action from misdemeanor to felony status by flipping over the tables of the money changers, crying out: "Stop turning my Father's house into a market!" (John 2:16).

I don't know if Jesus was opposed to all commercial activity in the temple or if He was simply angry that the religious authorities were making worship too expensive for the poor. When asked to justify the outburst, Jesus just said, "Destroy this temple, and I will raise it again in three days" (v. 19).

This must have been confusing for the disciples. Jesus taught them to love their enemies and turn the other cheek. But He also incited a riot in the temple. What gives?

Even though it might look like He threw a temper tantrum, Jesus didn't lose control that day in the temple. Quite the opposite: He showed that Someone was controlling Him. The only story we know about Jesus's teenage years was also set in Jerusalem during Passover. When it was time to leave, Mary and Joseph started for home—then realized they couldn't find Jesus anywhere. They went back to Jerusalem and eventually discovered Him in the temple courts, "sitting among the teachers, listening to them and asking them questions" (Luke 2:46). Every person listening to Him was "amazed at his understanding and his answers" (v. 47). Mary and Joseph weren't impressed. They wanted to know why He ran away. Jesus answered, "Didn't you know I had to be in my Father's house?" (v. 49).

Boom. Jesus's life was singularly focused on doing His Father's business. His Spirit was controlled by the will of the Father. Everything He did was for Him. With that perspective, we can understand His violent actions as consistent with His runaway actions in that same place years earlier. He was doing His Father's work. One instance called for Him to debate while another called for Him to be irate.

Self-control is not about managing ourselves but allowing God to manage us. Jesus was so filled with the Spirit of God that He did what the Spirit led in every circumstance. Sometimes that meant embracing a leper while other times it meant flipping over tables. One time Jesus rejected His own family's request to speak to Him, saying only that anyone who did the will of His Father was His true family (Matt. 12:46–50). Jesus wasn't always nice. But He was always in control, because God controlled Him. He had passion, but His passion didn't have Him.

⟳ GO IN

Who Is in Control?

My dad stands in line at the bank. It is 12:33 and he's due back at the office at 1:00. Three of the tellers close their windows at the same time. The customer ahead of him fills out an application for a credit card while providing the teller with the intimate details of every show she's bingeing on Netflix. 12:47. Dad feels the back of his neck grow hot. Sweat appears on his brow. The music playing over the speakers starts to bug him. The person behind him is standing too close, his bad breath only making Dad's neck hotter. It feels like the bank's AC cut out. 12:51 and the woman is still filling out the credit card application.

At 12:53 Dad makes it to the teller's window. His palms are sweaty, his heart is pounding, and his mouth is parched. He's mad at the bank. He's mad at the military for only giving him an hour for lunch. Now that he thinks about it, he's mad that the fries he crammed down at lunch had so much salt on them. Basically, he's mad at everyone and everything. He is on the verge of losing control because he's looking only to himself for self-control.

We've all been there—walking through our days trying to keep everything together on willpower alone. We tell ourselves to take a deep breath or a walk around the block. We hit up the next yoga class or log off social media for a day. And it helps. Sometimes. There are an infinite number of ways to calm down and maintain our self-control. The problem with relying on willpower for our self-control is that willpower is just that: ours.

See the problem?

Think of the times you've been in situations like my dad had at the bank. Times when you were stuck in traffic or waiting on hold. These mundane moments should be no big deal. And yet they have the power to send us into a rage. Left to our own devices, we will find ourselves frustrated by our circumstances. I don't care how zen we become, our willpower will never provide enough soul power. Only God can do that.

Self-control ultimately comes down to whom we cede control of our lives. Will we choose ourselves and our ever-changing willpower or the One for whom all things are possible (Phil. 4:13)?

Think of how many problems are caused by the lack of self-control. We eat too much candy or drink too much beer. We don't go to bed on time, so we can't get to work on time, which leaves us out of a good job most of the time. Can you hear me on this one, friends? I don't know anyone who doesn't want to have more self-control. Who among us wouldn't have a better life if we didn't get ticked off by a delayed flight or a petty insult from a stranger?

But nothing is scarier than feeling out of control. This is why people are afraid of surgery or air travel. In theory, we trust trained professionals like doctors and pilots, but we get scared because in those situations we're clearly not in control. But the truth is that we control very little in the rest of our lives too. The only thing we really control is whether or not we allow God to have control.

We must relinquish control and trust that God will provide all the control we need. It doesn't have to be scary, because "God gave us a spirit not of fear but of power and love and self-control" (2 Tim. 1:7 ESV). When we understand that God is in control *and* He's given us His Spirit to reject fear, we can live with an inner sense of control and confidence.

Consider Paul's ability to remain faithful while imprisoned by the Romans. Despite his dire circumstances, Paul ministered to the guards who kept him locked up. How does a prisoner do that? Only by the Spirit of God! Left to his own power, Paul would have likely grown bitter and hateful toward his captors.

Instead, he showed them the love of God and led them to the saving grace of Christ.

Is God in Control?

I saw a post recently that basically said: "You make 35,000 decisions per day. How many of them will you make with God?" Great question! If you want to know what your priorities are, you need only look at your calendar and your bank account. How you spend your time and money will reveal what you value in life. How do you know if you're allowing God to control your life? By asking yourself how often you consult God with your decisions.

Who decides how you respond to life? You or the Spirit of God? Do you simply do what you want and react based on however you feel? Or do you actively seek out God's counsel throughout the day? God listens and responds to our prayers. He longs to pour out His Spirit upon us so we can live an abundant life. But for a teacher to be effective in a student's life, the student must be willing to listen to and consult with his or her teacher. Christian self-control is not about finding a way to remain calm all the time. It's about knowing, on the deepest level, that our outer circumstances don't have to control our actions because we are controlled by the Spirit working in our inner lives.

There's a reason I'm still sporting an old, worn-out WWJD bracelet. Remember those from back in the day? I still rock mine because I need this reminder every day. I see those letters and I know that Jesus is ready and willing to guide me in the direction I need to go. I don't need to know everything Jesus did in the Bible to know how to act today. All I have to do is open my heart to the Holy Spirit and trust that whatever I ask for I will be given. I think that's even in the Bible somewhere!

START with ANGER, END with SELF-CONTROL

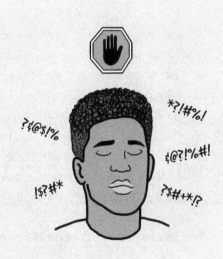

Controlled by the Spirit

Ceding control of your life to God is not easy. We all struggle to hand over full control because it's scary. But let's be honest. Wouldn't it be scarier to try to remain in control? How good of a job are you currently doing controlling your life? Are you making stellar decisions at work, keeping calm under pressure, and steering your life in the right direction? Or could you use a course correction? When difficult circumstances arise, are you white-knuckling your decisions by your own willpower?

When you hand over control to God, the Holy Spirit will immediately make a difference. When the Spirit is inside us, He will flow out from us. It's been said that difficult circumstances don't make a person so much as they reveal what's on the inside. When the pressure is on, if I rely only on myself apart from God, I don't know what the results will be. But if the Holy Spirit is in control, I know exactly what's going to flow out: genuine self-control.

I'm a genuine control freak who must return to the words Jesus prayed in the Garden of Gethsemane all the time. Do you recall what happened that night, the night He was betrayed? Jesus was deeply troubled, and He retreated into a private garden on the Mount of Olives to pray. There He wrestled with the coming events. Place yourself there. Really imagine what that must have been like. He was only thirty-three years old and in the prime of His life and career . . . and yet His death drew near. And not just any death awaited Him, but crucifixion, the worst kind of death imaginable. As He prayed, the Bible says He experienced *agony*— a word in Greek that was used to describe a soldier experiencing total fear in battle. Luke says His prayer became so intense that

"His sweat became like great drops of blood falling down to the ground" (Luke 22:44 NKJV). This certainly surpasses standing in line at the bank or being frustrated because our Wi-Fi is moving slowly. Jesus was at an absolute breaking point. If there was ever a moment He might genuinely lose self-control or turn away from the will of God, it would've been there in that garden.

But that's not what He did. Instead of panicking or giving in to His fear, He leaned harder into the Father in prayer. He kept His heart open to God and His will under God's control. Even as His disciples around Him slept, He continued to pray, ultimately saying those famous words: "not my will, but yours be done" (v. 42). Jesus's willpower told Him to leave the garden. He wanted the cup to pass from Him, but He was able to submit to the will of God because He trusted that all would be well in the end. That didn't mean He wouldn't suffer. That didn't mean He wouldn't die. What it meant was that He remained faithful to God's plan and will, not His own. Controlled by His Father, He walked into that garden in utter agony but emerged at peace and ready to finish the task.

TAKING THE NEXT STEP

PAUSE AND PONDER

Self-control is much more than an invisible virtue;
it's a key ingredient that validates and sustains
our inner plea for healthy and holy living.

PRESS INTO PRAYER

God is the greatest writer; He bled words
onto a page at the expense of His precious Son.
The people who hate Jesus trample on the pages of
   Scripture.
And the ones who love Jesus will embrace the sword
that cuts deep into the reader's heart to heal and satisfy
anyone willing to accept its open-heart surgery
that revives and brings to life all who read it.
The alive and active Word of God.
Come to life. Watch the old you die.
Beloved, joyfully lay your heart on the operating table
and allow the living Word that saved you
to be the living Word that shapes you.

Lord,

   Help remind us how deeply we need You. We can't control our circumstances, but we can control our attitude with the help of the Holy Spirit. Take away all the chaos we can't conquer on our own—which is all of it. We give it all to You, heavenly Father.

PROVE TO BE A PRACTICAL PIONEER

Self-control says no to sinful desires even when it hurts. What are some things you can say no to today?

8

Joy

The secret to joy is to keep seeking God where we doubt He is.

ANN VOSKAMP, *ONE THOUSAND GIFTS*

You will show me the path of life;
In Your presence is fullness of joy;
At Your right hand are pleasures forevermore.

PSALM 16:11 NKJV

↑ GO UP

Lies of Depression

Last summer, my wife and I went through a difficult season in our marriage. It seemed like we found ourselves in what we call "intense fellowship" (arguments) nearly every day. Denisse was eight months pregnant during this time, which didn't make anything easier. The issue that kept coming up was this: she felt lonely because I was working so much. I thought I was doing the right thing by providing for my family, but Denisse helped me see that I had once again put ministry before my marriage. But I'm thickheaded, so this took some time to sink in.

After one particularly intense fellowship session, I left the house and headed for Barnes & Noble, hoping to find some words of wisdom in the bookstore that might help our situation. I made my way to the Christian Living section, looking for a book that could make me a better husband. Even though it was a tough season, my prayer life was vibrant and my Bible reading was consistent. Now I needed some practical advice. I probably should have called my mentor, Shawn, but I was nervous about letting him know just how rough things in our marriage had gotten. Fortunately, I came across *Choosing Marriage*, a book by Debra Fileta. I had recently connected with her on social media and then over email. What were the odds? I flipped open the book to page 135 and started reading. Debra's words hit me head-on like a semitruck.

> One of the saddest stories I've ever heard was about a beautiful young woman who leapt to her death from the ninth floor of a parking garage. But the most shocking part of the story is this: no one saw it coming. Looking at her social media account, no one would have guessed this 19-year-old University of Pennsylvania track star was dealing with her own demons. Her "perfect-posted" life would have never tipped you off. Just one hour before she killed herself, she posted a beautiful picture on Instagram of twinkling lights in the city, with the backdrop of a beautiful sunset coming in from behind. What no one knew then is that the sun was about to set on her own young life.[1]

I closed the book and started weeping. I understood. My life wasn't nearly as perfect as I'd portrayed it to be online. So many of my battles had been waged in secret, with all my skeletons tucked neatly away. This pattern was now playing itself out in my marriage. I was pushing Denisse away, isolating myself, trying to handle everything on my own, and it wasn't working. I was terribly lonely and it was eating me alive.

Humans can survive about a week without water and two weeks without food. I'm convinced that relationship is the one thing we really can't go without, not even for a few hours, before it starts to take its toll on our soul. Loneliness is the toughest of all sorrows, the most cruel of all suffering. I drove home and confessed my loneliness to my wife, and she embraced me through my tears and brokenness. Hidden anger was exposed, forgiven, and released.

I have struggled with depression for years. There are many negative aspects, but one of the worst is loneliness. God designed us for relationship, and when we are cut off from it we feel as though there is no reason to live. Depression, if left untreated, destroys lives.

Do you struggle with depression? I don't have any perfect answer that will protect you from this horrible darkness. But what I can do is tell you what I know to be true about God and what has helped me during my more difficult days.

First, *it's okay to not be okay.* Pretending I am joyful when depressed has never helped my depression. It's okay to be honest with yourself, God, and others. God isn't scared of your pain. God is big enough to handle it, no matter how dark it feels. Jesus came for the sick, not the ones who have it perfectly together. If you struggle to get out of bed in the morning, He came for you. If you cancel plans with friends at the last second, He came for you. If you have to see a therapist every week, He came for you.

If you need medicine to keep the panic attacks away, He came for you. As my buddy Ryan always says, "There is no weakness in asking for help, only strength."

Second, *depression is a liar.* Depression says we aren't good enough, that we're a failure, and that we'll never measure up or truly matter to anyone. This deadly bully wants us to believe our lives are a complete loss. None of this is true, of course, but when we're depressed it's very hard to believe differently. When we're depressed, it's critical to remind ourselves that we can't always trust ourselves or our thoughts.

Third, *remaining in God's Word keeps truth in our hearts.* If depression is venom, then God's Word is the antidote. Nobody, not even depression, gets to tell us who we are. Only God has that right. My bad days are not the days that get to define my life. My life is defined by who God says I am, which is righteous and perfect (2 Cor. 5:21; Heb. 10:14).

When the darkness of depression comes knocking, reading God's Word might not be all we need. Therapy and doctors and community are important. But God's Word is the most important thing we need, because it always speaks truth in the face of depression's lies.

Depression Is the Dog That Lies

Depression slowly eats up every thought of every
minute and hour.
Depression quietly crawls,
sniffing, smelling, and scratching
at every inch of our souls,
moving like a dog finding the perfect place to *lie.*
It rolls over and digs around,
like a K-9 looking for his treat in the dirt.

It's sniffing out fertile soil to bury itself
in the depths of your soul, and it *lies* at the doorsteps of
    your mind.
Beloved, lock the doggy door.
Choose joy over being unfazed by the truth and
    damaged by lies.

Defining Joy

I find *joy* harder to define than other fruit of the Spirit. Is it just a synonym for happiness, or is it something more permanent? Kay Warren defines joy as "the settled assurance that God is in control of all the details of my life, the quiet confidence that ultimately everything is going to be all right, and the determined choice to praise God in all things."[2] According to that definition, joy comes from God in and through our decision to trust Him. To me, that means I can choose joy no matter what is happening in my life.

Recently I saw an incredible example of someone choosing joy in spite of difficult circumstances. Stephen Colbert, host of the *Late Show*, was being interviewed by Anderson Cooper on CNN, and he was talking about losing his father and brothers as a young boy. Stephen is the youngest of eleven children, and when he was ten years old, his father and two brothers died in a plane crash. In the interview, Cooper pressed Colbert as to whether he truly believed that even the worst events in life should be viewed as gifts, a view Colbert had stated in a prior interview. Colbert, a professing Christian, replied, "Yes. It's a gift to exist, and with existence comes suffering. There's no escaping that. I don't want it to have happened. I want it to *not* have happened, but if you are grateful for your life—which I think is a positive thing to do, not everybody is, and I am not always but it's the most positive thing to do—then you have to be grateful for all of it. You can't pick and choose what you're grateful for."[3] *That* is how you choose joy.

Discovering Joy

Do you know how amazing you are to God? Well, not because of what you have or don't have or what you have or haven't done. We are special because we are His beloved. The Bible says that we were made in His image and likeness. Buried within us are the many attributes of God. Most of us know God is love, but did you know God is also joy? This means we were made for joy. Yes, life is hard, but it's supposed to be joyful too!

We don't often realize this because we spend our time chasing after false joy, which is poison to the soul. There's no genuine joy outside the joy of the Lord. We find ourselves looking to created things rather than our Creator for our joy. All the joy on the face of the planet is derived from God. And there is no joy apart from God. All the attempts we make to find joy in things like traveling and consumerism are downright bankrupt because joy can only be found in God. Created things only produce momentary happiness. The Creator provides eternal joy.

Discovering the joy God has poured out in you can be tough if you don't believe the right stuff. Do you believe your heavenly Father branded joy into your DNA? Where do you believe true, lasting joy can be found? I will tell you. Look inside and not outside. Look to Jesus and not to everyone and everything this world offers. The world is crowded with desperate people thirsting for joy. Believe me. I was the chief joy-seeker. Sadly, many people settle for contaminated water and shut themselves off to the fountain of living water that never runs dry: Jesus Himself. Below are a few things the Bible says about who we are and what God has done for us:

1. Thankfully, the God of all joy laments over the unwise choices we tend to make: "My people have committed two evils: they have forsaken me, the fountain of living waters, and hewed out cisterns for themselves, broken cisterns that can hold no water" (Jer. 2:13 NKJV). Is your soul thirsty? You don't have to turn to social media, sex sites, or entertainment to see what they are saying about quenching your thirst. You don't drink out of the nearest puddle. Run to the reservoir that never stops flowing. Jesus is the overflowing fountain of joy you were made for. Drink deeply of the river of God. He is constantly refreshing, eternally satisfying, and infinitely pure. He will never leave you thirsty, discontent, and ill.

   Happiness from the wrong fountain can be deceptive. *But here's more good news for you: you can trust Jesus fully.* He's worthy of your trust, and He offers you this: "If anyone thirsts, let him come to me and drink. Whoever believes in me, as the Scripture has said, 'Out of his heart will flow rivers of living water'" (John 7:37–38 NKJV).

2. God created the world in His joy. God's plans for His children are joyful. He wants all His children to experience His abundant joy. He sent His Son to redeem us so we could again be in touch with Him and receive His joy. Jesus left heavenly royalty to come down to earthly poverty and say, "I've told you these things for a purpose: that my joy might be your joy, and your joy wholly mature" (15:11 MSG).

The Right Perspective

> I know what it is to be in need, and I know what it is to have plenty. I have learned the secret of being content in any and every situation, whether well fed or hungry, whether living in plenty or in want. I can do all this through him who gives me strength. (Phil. 4:12–13)

When I was a teenager, my parents bought a new car and decided to give me their "old" car, which just happened to be a fully loaded Lexus GS300. It sat on twenty-inch rims, had TV screens in the back of the seats, and included every other luxury add-on you could imagine. I was beside myself with excitement—until a few weeks later, when they asked for the car back. They didn't like their new car and sold it, which meant they needed their old car, or what I thought of as "my car," back. I was mad. You can't give a teenager a loaded Lexus and then expect him to drive a beat-up Camry! But that's what happened.

Before my parents bought the Lexus, I didn't even know what a Lexus was. But now I was bitter that I wasn't driving a Lexus. It's all about perspective. Nothing takes away our joy faster than a bad perspective. All of life is a gift. We must be grateful for everything we have and not focus on what we don't have. I went so quickly from not even knowing what a Lexus was to being angry I didn't have one. How messed up is that?

We all do this. Something makes us happy and then we feel as though we can't live without it. The truth is that we don't actually need anything on this planet except the loving presence of God. We must keep our expectations in check. Joy will never be found in anything outside God. Jesus Himself had "no place to lay his head" (Matt. 8:20). He walked this earth not in search of fame or security but rather His priority was staying close to the Father and doing His work. Our mission must be the same. We can't let our souls settle for substitutes. A Lexus won't make us joyful. Trust me.

Philippians is often seen as the most joyful book in the Bible, yet it was written from prison. Your circumstances don't determine your joy, your perspective does.

Named Beloved

It's easy for our thoughts to remain fixed on the past, worried by what we don't have or haven't become. That's the recipe for a joyless life. We need mental discipline to keep our thoughts constantly focused on God. We must have filtered thinking instead of filthy thinking. This is hard since the media throws negativity toward us all day, every day. But without cultivating our joy, one mental decision at a time, we will never grow tough enough in Christ to live a joy-filled life.

Be mindful of your mind's focus, and your whole life will change. Your God-given dreams will become clearer, you'll experience spiritual maturity, and you'll be contagiously joyful instead of a contagion. When you keep your eyes fixed on Jesus, you'll find the joy in everyone and every circumstance.

When my mental muscles are weak, my thinking becomes random. When I'm not focused on God, I become easily discouraged because I'm spiritually malnourished. We've all been there. Being lazy in your thought life will affect you and everyone around you. It starts with your private thoughts and then inevitably comes out in your actions when tough circumstances arise.

We tend to think of discipline as a negative thing. But a life without disciplined thinking is a destructive life waiting to happen. Of course, your thinking will never be perfect while you are dressed up in your flesh. Perfection only wore skin once, and His name was and is Jesus. For you and me, it's less about perfection and more about progression. It's not about being flawless, instead it's about chasing excellence. God delights in His children and their improvement. We can improve our thought lives, one day at a time. Consider Paul's words to the Philippians: "Finally, brothers and sisters, whatever is true, whatever is noble, whatever is right, whatever is pure, whatever is lovely, whatever is admirable—if anything is excellent or praiseworthy—think about such things" (4:8).

When you think right, you will live right. And when you live right, you'll live in the present and not the past. No matter your name. No matter where you're from. No matter what you've done. No matter where you live. No matter how many mistakes you've made. I'd love to convince you that you can discover the joy that comes in finding freedom in Christ. You aren't confined to the words people have said about you, nor are you defined by the lies of this world.

You may have been labeled with names that reflect who you used to be. But God has your true name written in His book. When you come to faith in Jesus Christ, all things become new—even your joy. When joy comes, the jabs from the journey disappear.

You are no longer "the liar."

You are no longer "the cheater."

You are no longer "the trash talker."

You are no longer "the whore."

You are no longer "the addict."

You are no longer "the punk."

Your new name is "His beloved." You belong to God as His precious child. No matter how good or bad you feel. God sees you through the beautiful lens of His Son's perfection. He looks beyond your reputation and your sins toward the finished work of Jesus. We can rejoice and be filled with joy. We don't have to be stuck in the past because we serve a merciful God who looks past our past.

Joy for the Journey

> Consider it pure joy, my brothers and sisters, whenever you face trials of many kinds. (James 1:2)

Dietrich Bonhoeffer was a Lutheran pastor who refused to submit to Hitler's racist regime during WWII. Despite the threat of imprisonment and death, Bonhoeffer spoke out boldly against Hitler's discrimination and worked hard, albeit underground, to continue training young pastors in the true way of Christ when many other Christians were being led astray. To spread the gospel during this time, Bonhoeffer wrote secret letters of encouragement and theological guidance to roughly 150 pastors.

Many of those pastors were arrested and executed for keeping the faith. During the winter of 1942, mere months before Bonhoeffer himself would be arrested and executed, he wrote one last letter to the pastors, many of whom were severely downtrodden. What does a pastor do or say in such an awful situation? How does one sing boldly of the faith when the whole world seems to be crumbling around them? Bonhoeffer could have written a disheartened letter, and nobody would have blamed him. But that's not what he did.

He began by listing the names of the most recent pastors who had been martyred. He then said this about them:

Everlasting joy shall be upon their heads. We are glad for them; indeed, should we say that we sometimes secretly envy them? . . . Serve the Lord with joy . . . for this our life has been given to us, and for this it has been preserved for us unto the present hour. This joy, which no one shall take from us, belongs not only to those who have been called home but also to us who are alive. We are one with them in this joy, but never in melancholy. How are we going to be able to help those who have become joyless and discouraged if we ourselves are not borne along by courage and joy? Nothing contrived or forced is intended here, but something bestowed and free.[4]

Bonhoeffer encouraged the pastors to open themselves to God, who has known every kind of agony—from the manger to the cross—and yet is the very embodiment of joy. There is nothing we experience in life, he argued, that God does not understand and has not already overcome. Thus, no matter what circumstances we face, we can draw from the joy of God. What encouraging words from a man in such a discouraging place! Bonhoeffer himself would soon be taken from his fiancée, imprisoned, beaten, and driven to such a desolate place in his heart and mind that he considered suicide. And yet, when it came time to die, by hanging, he preached a final sermon to the inmates in prison, saying, in part: "This is for me the end, the beginning of life."[5]

Wow. Those are the words of a man who knew internal joy. He could thus endure any life experience. This is the kind of joy God makes available to all of us. The kind that allows a man imprisoned and executed by the Nazis to never lose heart, even though he struggled, because he understood that God, who is joy, never abandoned him and would deliver him—if not in this life, then the next.

God Has Given Enough

Trusting that God has given us enough grace for any circumstance ought to produce abiding joy in us. We have what we need. My dear friend Dave knows and loves Jesus. He was recently diagnosed with brain cancer. Dave already knows a lot about suffering because he watched his teenage daughter die from a car accident. He once said to me, "Suffering isn't always the easiest route to good, but suffering can be profoundly good. Suffering can breed selfishness and bitterness, which can crush and break a family into pieces. Or it can deeply unite and tightly pull them together through hardships." What Dave understands is that we have a choice to make when we suffer. Will it overcome us, or will we believe what Bonhoeffer believed, that God has already overcome and we can thus be joyful?

If we choose to abide in Christ, nothing can suppress our joy.

No sickness.
No darkness.
No hardship.
No broken relationships.
Nothing.

Nothing robs us of our joy faster than the utter hopelessness that springs from hardships, and nothing encourages our joy more than a heart that remains desperate for Jesus even when tragedy strikes. The key to lasting, abiding joy is intimacy. This joy doesn't just come from knowing Jesus but is a sweet fruit that grows through abiding in Him. "Remain in me, as I also remain in you. No branch can bear fruit by itself; it must remain in the vine. Neither can you bear fruit unless you remain in me" (John 15:4).

Notice the word *remain* (aka *abiding*) occurs about four times in one line. By our abiding in Him and He in us, His joy will always be in us. Dave's joy wasn't just an intermittent experience but a permanent one. It was never dampened by his circumstances. He understood the words Jesus spoke over his disciples: "Now is your time of grief, but I will see you again and you will rejoice, and no one will take away your joy" (16:22).

All of Christ's followers back in the day passed through many tragedies, trials, and tests, but He told them nothing could rob them of their joy—His joy in them. Nada!

Take a moment to consider these three illustrations of the abiding nature of Christian joy, and ponder the fact that Christ's joy in us is unaffected by our outward circumstances and conditions.

1. Joy in the jaws of death. As we have seen, our Lord experienced this joy in the shadow of the cross (John 15:11).
2. Joy in Jesus, not the junkyard. We are not to let our joy depend upon anything earthly or temporary but "rejoice that [our] names are written in heaven" (Luke 10:20).
3. Joy in the jailhouse. Paul and Silas, though in great trouble in prison, were filled with Christ's own joy that enabled them to sing praises at midnight (Acts 16:25).

It is an astonishing and a wonderful thing that true Christian joy is not only untouched by adverse circumstances but it is actually championed by such trials and tests. "Consider it pure joy, my brothers and sisters, whenever you face trials of many kinds" (James 1:2). Joy is about perspective. Joy focuses on the *triumph* of the cross, not the *trials* of many kinds. It becomes a deep, slow river of inexpressible hope that we can freely give, give, and *give*.

START with DEPRESSION, END with JOY

⊕ REACH OUT

Defend Your Joy

Several years ago, I was blocked on Twitter by an outspoken atheist. It was Super Bowl Sunday, and I had just left a party where some dude spilled a drink on my fresh-out-of-the-box Chuck Taylors. I wasn't in the best of moods. That doesn't excuse my behavior, but here's what happened.

I left the party and jumped on Twitter. After scrolling through my feed, I tweeted: *Sometimes I really wish I could just slap some sense into a drunk. Maybe it'll teach them some respect. Lord, help me.*

That was how I felt in the moment, but my tweet lacked any kind of compassion. I honestly didn't think much about the tweet. I was just blowing off some steam. I thought it would be harmless. Moments later I realized it was much more than that.

I began scrolling through the responses to the tweet, most of which were laughter. Then I received a direct message that stopped me in my tracks: *DUDE. You call yourself a Christian? This is why I left the church a long time ago. You guys are smiley face hypocrites.*

Instantly I realized how right this guy was and how wrong I had been to tweet that. I frantically wanted to reply. But first I took a closer look at his own Twitter feed. There were a lot of tweets about his dislike of fake people and "poser" Christians. He liked to quote well-known atheists as well. I scrolled further and read a courageous post about his own struggles with depression. I don't normally Twitter-stalk people like this, but I felt awful for what I had done. So I kept reading. It became really clear to me that this guy had been in some real-life spiritual battles.

Surely my tweet had hurt him in the same way other "poser Christians" had.

Worried, but not wanting to seem too serious, I punched out a reply: *Bro, don't take your Super Bowl fury out on me, better luck next year. Lol JK man sorry.*

He quickly replied: *You should really practice what you preach on social media. Have some empathy. What would Jesus do?*

That's when my baby Christian came out. I couldn't handle the criticism. Instead of apologizing, I logged out of Twitter, deleted the app from my phone, and cried out to Jesus. I asked God's grace to change me. I confessed that I had become cynical and was in desperate need of God's joy in my life.

Stress doesn't just steal our joy, it also provokes us to sin. I was in a bad mood and had taken my eyes off Jesus. The next thing I knew, I had no empathy, no compassion, and no love for this guy on Twitter who needed all three of those things from me.

I remember lying on the floor, staring at the ceiling and not wanting to face this dilemma. However, all of this tension began to grow too heavy on my conscience. I cracked open my Bible and flicked the pages to 1 Peter 4:8: "Love covers a multitude of sins," or in other words, forgives and disregards the offenses of others. The Bible also commands us to make allowances for one another (Eph. 4:2). In essence, we are to joyfully allow people to be less than perfect.

It all started to click. I'm really quick to rejoice when others allow me to be the messy human that I am, but sadly I'm naturally bent toward jabbing people with judgment instead of joyfully extending grace when others spill their dirt on me. How sad is that? I wasn't facing anything like Bonhoeffer faced, and yet I allowed the enemy to take a foothold in my heart and direct my actions toward sin. But if we truly commit ourselves to having a sincere faith in Jesus Christ, and allow God's promises to bring us the peace that "transcends all understanding" (Phil. 4:7), we will be filled with a glorious joy that will conquer any temptation to sin.

The key to victory is *activity*. Love is action. It was time for me to become love. I took initiative. I re-downloaded the app. I reached up to God in prayer and then *I reached out again*. Defending our joy takes demonstrating His love, even when it's tough.

I reconnected with my critic, and we eventually jumped on a phone call and gently talked through our differences. "A soft answer turns away wrath" (Prov. 15:1 NKJV). It became evident to me that my calling was to become a peacemaker and not a peace breaker. What the enemy means for our harm, God intends for our good. Doing what's right will always give us the courage to joyfully reach out.

Dance for Joy

I can remember being so hyped about visiting Disneyland when I was a child. Many people called Disneyland "the happiest place on earth," and so I was ready to experience the cosmic emotional high that comes with great food, gigantic rides, and carnival game music.

Let's do this! I thought. But though the moments were memorable and mesmerizing, Disneyland underdelivered on its enormous promise. The lines were crazy long and that day was hotter than a track meet in Mozambique. We had to wait almost a full hour to enjoy a single ride that would only last a few minutes.

I tell you this memory only to say that dancing from happiness doesn't compare to dancing for joy. Happiness is momentary, but joy is eternal. People who delight in God can't help but dance for joy whether they are at Disneyland or in a Nazi concentration camp.

TAKING THE NEXT STEP

PAUSE AND PONDER

There's no joy outside of Jesus. My joy will always be at risk when I depend on another person or thing for it.

PRESS INTO PRAYER

God's grace is the boxing gloves of the fighter named
    Freedom.
Freedom wore the stripes that would save our lives.
Where the opponent named Sin looked big, God's grace
    was bigger.
Instead of standing in a ring, Freedom wore nail-pierced
    rings in His hands.
The joy that was set before Him enabled Him to endure
    the cross.
The cost was paid in full.
Jesus is freedom; He is your freedom.
Beloved,
let the freedom to fail give you the hope to fight.
Hope already won the war.
Keep on fighting for your joy!

Lord,
    My days lately have been flooded with darkness; I feel like I'm
drowning, and I can't keep my head above the waters. I pray that

You calm the waters of my heart as You whisper Your truth to still the waves of my soul and teach me how to trust You again. I pray that my joy that has been taken from me be restored.

PROVE TO BE A PRACTICAL PIONEER

With Jesus, anyone can go from hopeless to joyful in a single moment. He's the only One who has the ability to wrap His eternal hands around you and constantly hug your soul. Take a moment to share this hope with your spouse, friends, or coworkers.

9

Kindness

Therefore, as God's chosen people, holy and dearly loved, clothe yourselves with compassion, *kindness*, humility, gentleness and patience.

COLOSSIANS 3:12, EMPHASIS ADDED

Not all of us can do great things. But we can do small things with great love.

MOTHER TERESA

Don't Be Afraid!

A lot of words come to mind when people think of God, but
kindness is not often one of them. People are far more likely to be
afraid of God than they are to think of Him as kind. We need to be
reminded that God is not just loving, He is also kindhearted. He
wants to embrace us with His kindness. We can misunderstand
His nature so badly. An unkind God doesn't make laughter. An

unkind God doesn't make art. An unkind God doesn't make an entire universe of beauty for us to enjoy.

But *kind* is different from *nice*. One can be nice without being kind. A nice person smiles and tells us what we want to hear. A kind person tells us, in love, what we need to hear. Take Paul, for instance. He wasn't always the nicest guy. He could be rather blunt at times. But he was kind. When he wrote to the church in Corinth, he listed kindness as one of the spiritual fruits God had developed in him as proof that he was a genuine apostle of Christ (2 Cor. 6:1–13). Paul wasn't always touchy-feely, but he was kind—just like God.

The Ten Commandments

Believe it or not, one of God's greatest kindnesses to us is a clear set of boundaries on the best way for us to live. Consider the Ten Commandments—here's a recap from Exodus 20:1–17:

1. I am the LORD your God. You shall have no other gods before Me.
2. You shall not make for yourself an idol.
3. You shall not misuse the name of the LORD your God.
4. Remember the Sabbath day by keeping it holy.
5. Honor your father and your mother.
6. You shall not murder.
7. You shall not commit adultery.
8. You shall not steal.
9. You shall not give false testimony.
10. You shall not covet.

The Ten Commandments are intense; they don't mince words. They set a high standard for how we are to live. They're not nice.

Nor was Jesus when He made the Ten Commandments even more difficult in His Sermon on the Mount, telling us God will judge us not according to our actions but instead according to the condition of our hearts. I mean, which is easier? Not committing adultery or not lusting after someone? Jesus said that if we lust in our hearts it's the same as if we had committed the act of adultery itself. Nothing nice about that! But . . . it is kind.

Why is that?

Because these laws are good for us. If we keep them, we will live more godly and peaceful lives, and that is the very purpose of kindness. God is kind to us because God wants what is best for us.

We see God's kindness more clearly in light of our darkness.

We are all sinful. Romans 5:12 says, "Sin came into the world through one man, and death through sin, and so death spread to all men because of sin" (ESV). Basically, we are messy by birth; we are messy by nature; we are messy by actions. Sin is running wild in us everywhere from our genes to our hearts. If anyone says otherwise, just have them read the Ten Commandments.

Because of God's kindness and as a result of His mercy and love, He sent Jesus into our world to die on a cross for our sins. There is no surprise more fascinating than the shocking reality of being intimately loved that much, regardless of how long we chose to wallow in the mud.

Wallowing is an interesting word; it suggests the image of a pig wallowing in its muddy pen. We aren't pigs, but at times we can feel just as dirty as one. But don't fret; there's good news! God loves us too much to keep us in our mess.

God isn't distant from us, He's reaching out to us.

We hear David's heart when he was stuck in a low and messy place:

I waited patiently for the LORD;
>   he turned to me and heard my cry.
He lifted me out of the slimy pit,
>   out of the *mud and mire*;
he set my feet on a rock
>   and gave me a firm place to stand.
He put a new song in my mouth,
>   a hymn of praise to our God.
Many will see and fear the LORD
>   and put their trust in Him. (Ps. 40:1–3, emphasis added)

We want God to reach down and grab our hand, but first we have to cry out to Him. God turns suffering into songs of joy. He takes the humble from the slimy mud to the solid rock. God is kind, but He doesn't force His love on us. Nor does He force us to leave the low and muddy places. He refuses to violently drag us out of the filth by squeezing our ears and harshly calling us names. He created us as creatures of free will. By His kindness He has made His love available to us through His Son, Jesus, but we must take initiative to receive Him. Just as we are; not on our terms but on His. We can accept His love and begin to know Him personally. How? I'll take you through it.

First, Acknowledge Your Sin

All of us are sinners. "For all have sinned and fall short of the glory of God" (Rom. 3:23).

Yes! God's love is perfect. Everything about Him is perfect, including His justice and His holiness. Because He loves you, and He is kind, He wants to forgive you. But because He's also holy and just, He can't turn a blind eye to sin. The Bible says "the wages of sin is death" (6:23).

Here's the gospel in a nutshell again:

> For **G**od so loved the world
> that He gave His **O**nly
> begotten **S**on, that whoever believes
> in Him should not **P**erish
> but have **E**verlasting
> **L**ife.

Second, Repent of Your Sin

Imagine you're drowning in a pool. The only way you can call on a lifeguard to save you is to admit that you are drowning. In the same way, the only way you can call on Jesus Christ to save you is to admit that you are drowning in your sin. In order to do this, you have to see your sin as God sees it. Take a moment to think about it.

If you don't see yourself as truly lost in sin and wallowing in the mud, then there is no reason to believe you need to be cleansed by Christ. The biggest evidence that a person has a new life in Christ is simply a change of lifestyle. The easiest way to spot a person who is genuinely sorry about their old lifestyle is by seeing how different they are in their new one.

Finally, Accept God's Gift of Grace and Put Your Trust in the Savior

The entire message of this book is to *start where you are*. Grace meets you exactly where you are—but it doesn't leave you where it found you. God says, "I will give you a new heart and put a new spirit in you" (Ezek. 36:26). That's grace! Grace calls you out to change and then fills your heart with the power to pull it off. To accept God's grace and not put your trust in Jesus changes nothing in your life. A gift that you halfway receive is of no true value. God has paid the price for your sins yesterday, today, and tomorrow. But you must receive His gift of eternal life once and for all today.

It's available to you right now!

At this very moment, Christ says He is standing at the door of your heart waiting and knocking. "Behold, I stand at the door and knock. If anyone hears my voice and opens the door, I will come in" (Rev. 3:20 ESV).

Kindness Leads to Repentance

Rosaria Butterfield's memoir, *The Secret Thoughts of an Unlikely Convert*, details her journey from atheism to fully committed Christianity. In the book she describes publishing an article critiquing evangelical Christians, people she saw as judgmental and not very smart. She received a staggering number of responses, some of which were supportive and others quite the opposite. She says she organized the letters in two piles on her desk: hate mail on one side and fan mail on the other. Then one day she got a letter she couldn't place in either pile. It was from a pastor, and it was filled with curiosity, kindness, and difficult questions. Rosaria let the letter sit alone on her desk for seven days. Eventually she reached out to the pastor, and the pair became friends, a friendship that proved influential in her journey to faith.

Jesus used kindness to communicate His love and message to His disciples. As a rabbi, He was a distinguished figure in the community and could thus have acted like one, attending only the best dinner parties and keeping company with only others who held prestige. But time and again we are told in the Gospel narratives that He did just the opposite. Jesus was heavily criticized by other elites for eating with tax collectors and befriending prostitutes. Jesus could have simply preached at these nonentities and rebuked them for their sin. But He took time to be with them, to show them kindness through friendship. We serve a kind God. He does not call us servants but friends (John 15:15).

GO IN

We have all had those mornings. The alarm has been going off for half an hour while we press snooze. Finally we crawl out of bed and start rushing around, trying not to be late for work or school. But then we can't make up our minds about that most crucial decision: What on earth are we going to wear? Our closet is jam-packed. We have more than we need. Our thoughts race through the coming day. *What meetings do I have? How professional must I look? Who's going to see me? How much do I want to impress them?* You know you've been there! Being self-conscious about my outfit is always worse for me if I fell asleep the night before scrolling through social media, comparing my wardrobe to the influencers who seemingly have an unending supply of the latest fashions. It's not cool to have other people decide for you what you will wear. It's really not cool to have your insecurities do it.

Before we think about how we're going to dress ourselves physically, we ought to first consider our spiritual clothes. The good thing about this task is that it's easier than picking out an outfit. God has offered to dress us. He already knows exactly what we should wear and is prepared to put it on us. As Paul writes, "Therefore, as God's chosen people, holy and dearly loved, clothe yourselves with compassion, kindness, humility, gentleness and patience" (Col. 3:12). Notice what he is not saying. He is not saying we should put on the emotional burdens we carry with us from the day before, which is what most of us do. Our typical pattern is to wake up and put on fresh clothes—but leave on the emotional struggles and hurts from the day before. We concern ourselves far more with what's on the outside than what's on the inside. But Paul says we must first concern ourselves with what we're wearing on the inside. We need to put on compassion, kindness, humility, gentleness, and patience. These are the most important "clothes" we will wear! *The attitude we choose to wear will determine the type of fruit we bear.* I don't know about you, but I don't want yesterday's troubles to take away the promises God has for me today.

We must make this choice at the beginning of our day. Regardless of how we feel when we wake up, we get to choose what to clothe ourselves in. Will we be more concerned with our outer clothing or our inner clothing? We can only live out what is breathed into us by the Spirit of God. Galatians 5 speaks about *kindness* being a fruit of the Holy Spirit. It's an act that every believer is privileged to carry out. Kindness exudes from our lives when we are earnest about reflecting the character of Christ. People marvel at God's love when we clothe ourselves with kindness, but they run away from the odor of people-pleasing.

The Best Evidence Is Our Kindness

> Or do you show contempt for the riches of his kindness, forbearance and patience, not realizing that God's kindness is intended to lead you to repentance? (Rom. 2:4)

I love the bravado of a marine fresh out of basic training. I enjoy the cowboy culture of Oklahoma, the sacred wisdom of Native Americans, and I can't get enough of movies like *American*

Sniper. But all these pale in comparison to someone who displays simple kindness. Nothing is more powerful!

I take my small interactions with people seriously, no matter if I'm at Chick-fil-A or an important business meeting. Each moment is an opportunity to be clothed in kindness, which spreads God's love and leads others to the Lord. It's not about being nice and fake. It's about truly wanting everyone to be drawn closer to God and understanding that we can help make that happen by showing kindness to each person we meet—even the ones we meet every day.

A few months ago, Denisse and I got into a disagreement shortly before going to bed. Our plan was to visit a national park, but we couldn't decide on the best time to leave for the trip. We went back and forth about it until the conversation grew heated. We did exactly what Paul told us not to do: "let the sun go down on your anger" (Eph. 4:26 ESV).

I slept terribly, tossing and turning all night. Instead of praying and handing the situation over to the Lord, I tried to deal with it myself, and the enemy walked all over me.

The next morning I woke up even angrier than I'd been when I went to sleep. I rolled over, looked at my sleeping wife, and thought, *I'm sick and tired of arguing with you. You always have to be right. You don't understand me. You show me no respect. I'm so angry with you.*

That's when the Holy Spirit intervened, saying, *She's not your enemy. She's not your problem.* I grabbed my phone and opened my Bible app. The verse of the day was: "If God is for us, who can be against us?" (Rom. 8:31). The Holy Spirit convicted me that the "us" included my wife. It's not me versus her. We are in this thing together. I can't ever forget that we are a team. This is never about me; it's only ever about *we.* How we love one another for God's glory is what matters most. The Lord helped me in that moment to rectify my mistake from the night before. I chose not to clothe myself in yesterday's baggage but to put on kindness instead. As soon as Denisse woke up, I was ready with an apology.

We have to remember that our emotions are not always the best guides for our lives. Sometimes we are going to wake up in funky moods. If we allow our emotions to dictate our lives, we will forever be held hostage to however we are feeling. But if we instead clothe ourselves in the Holy Spirit, we will be directed by God's Spirit instead of the whims of our feelings. Make the decision today to put on kindness before you do anything. It makes all the difference.

REACH OUT

Rachelle was a joy-filled woman who used her great fortune for God's glory, generously giving away money whenever she could. Long before I came to Christ, I dated her daughter Amy. I was a terrible influence on Amy. Thinking about the damage I caused to both of our lives breaks my heart. One day we decided to take advantage of Rachelle's generosity because we wanted to go to New Orleans and party during the NBA All-Star weekend.

We drove to Rachelle's house, and I fed her the story we'd just made up. I said, "My grandma is seriously ill and might die soon. My father quit his job to care for her full-time. I honestly don't know how we're going to pay our bills this month. I hate to ask . . . but is there anything you might be able to do for us, Rachelle?"

Rachelle didn't blink. She wrote me a check for five thousand dollars, pushed it into my guilty hand, and said, "God bless you and your family."

We cashed the check the next day and booked our flights to New Orleans. When we got home, Amy's sister called to say she saw our trip photos on Facebook. Amy told her about the trip, but then also told her about the "financial trouble" my family was in and how Rachelle had helped us out.

Amy's sister actually knew my parents. I had no idea! She told Amy that she had recently seen my parents on their own vacation to Myrtle Beach. We begged Amy's sister not to tell Rachelle we had lied. But a few days later Amy's sister told her mom the truth. "Rashawn's family isn't broke," she said. "They didn't need your money. Rashawn and Amy stole it from you so they could party in New Orleans."

"They aren't about to lose their home?" Rachelle asked.

"No, Mom. They played you."

"Well," Rachelle said, smiling. "That's great news." She placed a hand over her heart. "I'm *so* happy to hear that his family is okay."

Doing Right When Wronged

Rachelle was so filled with the love of Christ that she loved us despite our betrayal. This story is so shameful for me to tell, but it's important. Rachelle epitomized the radical attitude Jesus calls us to have toward those who wrong us. Love in the face of hate brings God joy. No matter how dishonest or disloyal people are to us, God calls us to be kind to them just as He has been kind to us. Rachelle didn't condone my actions, but she saw beyond the surface level of my brokenness. She trusted that God wanted her to not worry about what happened with the money. She believed my family needed help, and she gave it.

We must see past the deceit, hypocrisy, and manipulation of our enemies. The sting of betrayal runs deep. But God tells us

START with SELFISHNESS, END with KINDNESS

to leave vengeance to Him. We, on the other hand, are called to love and be kind.

God can use people who hurt you to point you closer to His heart. When we are betrayed, we experience what Jesus Himself experienced. He was betrayed and wounded by those He loved the most. He understands what we are going through. Despite the betrayal, Jesus continued to love His enemies, even as He died on the cross for them.

Yesterday's Mess, Tomorrow's Message

Jesus's resurrected body carries the wounds He suffered in death. He didn't deny His wounds as part of His identity. He redeemed them. When Thomas wanted to know if Jesus was truly the Christ, he asked if he could touch Jesus's wounds. And Jesus let him. If we are to know each other, we must be willing to have our wounds seen and felt.

Without the pain of our past we don't have a purpose for our future. If we allow it, our struggles will reveal how strong God is. God will allow our enemies to *teach* us a lot more than they *take* from us. But we have to respond to them with kindness if we want this to happen. Jesus laid it out clearly: "Do good to them, and lend to them without expecting anything back. Then your reward will be great, and you will be children of the Most High, because he is *kind* to the ungrateful and wicked" (Luke 6:35–36, emphasis added).

I am not proud of what I did to Rachelle, but I am enormously grateful God used her to teach me how to respond to my enemies: with love and kindness.

TAKING THE NEXT STEP

PAUSE AND PONDER

God can use people who hurt you to
point you closer to His heart.
If we don't teach people who God is, this world
will teach them everything He isn't.

PRESS INTO PRAYER

God isn't angry like some stern police officer.
He is kind.
God's mercies never grow old.
His heart never darkens nor does it ever turn cold.
His kindness never runs out.
His disciplines are never ill-timed.
Certainly His love never dries up or suspiciously fades.

Lord,

Thank You for reminding me that kindness isn't weak; it's actually a weapon we should all use daily. Help me to love my enemies—and bless them beyond measure. Father, I can't win this battle without You. I thank You for allowing Your kindness to be a badge of honor I get to share with the world every single day in Jesus's name.

PROVE TO BE A PRACTICAL PIONEER

Who has hurt you? Grab your journal and write down every person who is hindering you from moving forward into the future God has for you. Pray for them. Find a way to respond with *kindness*. Your smallest acts of kindness will always be your biggest acts of love.

10

Goodness

Do you despise the riches of His *goodness*, forbearance, and longsuffering, not knowing that the *goodness* of God leads you to repentance?

ROMANS 2:4 NKJV, EMPHASIS ADDED

> I remain confident of this:
> I will see the goodness of the Lord
> in the land of the living.

PSALM 27:13

 COME UP

Is God Good?

In 1967, near the Texas coast, a drunken man beat his pregnant wife, sending her into preterm labor. She was rushed to the hospital, where she gave birth to a baby girl nearly four months too early. Miraculously, the child survived, but only after a grueling six and a half months in the hospital. The mother named the baby Renea, but the family affectionately nicknamed her Rat because of her smallness. When her mother first took her home from the hospital, she slept in a shoebox because she was so tiny! That little baby grew up strong and healthy and eventually became my mom.

Each time I remember her story, I am filled with both wonder and dread. The goodness of the Lord allowed my mom to survive, but my grandmother suffered horrible abuse that almost took her life, not to mention my mom's. Domestic violence is a horrible reality far too many people endure in this world. Abuse leaves many bewildered and unwilling or unable to believe in a good God.

Every Christian struggles with faith. It's just part of the faith journey. My struggles never had to do with believing God existed. It simply wasn't hard for me to imagine a God living in heaven who created this incredible earth. No, my struggle was believing this God was actually good. Because I was so broken myself, as were so many people around me, I had trouble believing anything good could come out of me or my circumstances. Combine these struggles with the abuse my mother and others I love suffered, and you had a recipe for suspicion toward the promise of a good and faithful God. God existed, sure, but maybe He was cold-hearted. How else could you explain all the suffering in the world?

Perhaps you've had this suspicion about God. You want to believe He is good, but your bad experiences make that difficult. A friend turned her back on you. A divorce blindsided you. Your dream school rejected you. Maybe your beloved child was taken by an illness. The Bible says, "He causes his sun to rise on the evil and the good, and sends rain on the righteous and the unrighteous" (Matt. 5:45), which is another way of saying bad things happen to good people. This is the consequence of sin. Every one of us, at some point, feels its devastating effects. Sin was not God's plan for the world, but when Adam and Eve chose to disobey God and rebel against His goodness they were exiled, and things only got worse from there. Soon after, one of Adam and Eve's sons murdered his own brother. We've been sinning and killing one another ever since.

We were made for so much more than sin. God created us by His love so we could live in it and from it. He longs for us to have peace with Him and one another. But sin makes it easy to feel alienated from God and each other. Yet here's the good news: God's goodness transcends the pollutions of this world. Before sin entered the picture, God said all of creation was good! And when we fell away from His goodness, He sent His Son, Jesus, to die for us in order to restore us to right relationship with God. So even though our world is infected with sin and our lives are messy because of it, God gets right in the middle of our mess. He reminds us that no matter what has happened in this life, He wants us to have what He's always wanted us to have: everlasting life with Him and in Him. This doesn't mean bad things won't happen. It does mean that God is forever unwilling to abandon us to the effects of our sin. He's that good!

Mercy for Our Mess

It took years, but now I know that God is good. Each day He reveals more of His goodness, and I fall deeper in love with Him. It's almost like a drug. God's presence never fails to bring me into a state of euphoria and satisfaction. It's not that I crave what God can give me; I want all of who God is. He's who I want. I don't want the blessings but the One who blesses. There is so much in our world that muddies our understanding of what is good. You might not realize what a blessing it is to be in the presence of God the first time, or even the first twenty times. But if you'll return to God's presence and continue to taste what He offers, I promise you there will be no turning back. You'll see that whatever goodness this world offers is nothing in comparison to God. And when the tougher days of life come along, you'll discover that suffering is sweet in the light of God's goodness.

Why Settle for Anything Less?

Remember the story I told you about my son Jerrell eating dirt instead of the sweet treat I wanted to give him? We can laugh at that sort of behavior, but I think we're just as guilty of confusing what is good with what is gross. We've been invited to the sacred and bountiful feast of a good God, and yet many of us choose to stay outside looking for our own meal. Why? Maybe it's because we doubt God is truly good. But here's the deal: God's sole desire is to do good things in and through the children who come to Him. That's all He wants for us. That's why the Bible tells us He is a good Father who gives His children what they need (Matt. 7:11). We don't deserve the good gifts of our Father. And yet He gives them anyway because He's infinitely good.

Every waking moment, we should be astonished at the goodness of God, stunned that He would bother to choose us and call us by name. He refuses to mass-produce His children and insists on weaving us together through an intimate process that constantly shapes us more deeply into His image. Our hands should stretch high for His glory and our jaws should drop low at His love. We should stand amazed that He uses every created thing to point toward Himself.

At the end of the day, there's one thing I know with all my heart: the goodness of God is *better* than anything this world has to offer.

> Better than our brokenness.
> Better than our self-righteousness.
> Better than our church attendance.
> Better than our marriages.
> Better than our greatest tithe record.
> Better than our latest award.
> Better than cash and sex.
> Better than every relationship, including an ex.
> Better than our last breath.
> Better than our first kiss.
> Better than Starbucks.
> Better than taco trucks.
> Better than a name or fame.
> Better than a lousy ol' video game.

Paradox of Person

When I look into my soul, I don't see goodness. I see paradox. I can see some good, sure, but I also see a whole lot of bad. Sometimes I feel like all I am is one big bundle of contradiction. I love and I hate. I have faith and I have doubts. I am infinitely hopeful and yet so easily discouraged. I am nothing if not conflicted! I take comfort in the fact that Paul felt this way too, and wrote, "For we know that the law is spiritual, but I am of the flesh, sold under sin. For I do not understand my own actions. For I do not do what I want, but I do the very thing I hate" (Rom. 7:14–15 ESV).

This side of heaven, we are going to battle sin and waffle back and forth between doing good and evil. I get depressed and I sing for joy. I am confident and fearful. Left to my own devices, I never really know what I'm going to get.

That said, we must accept the entirety of who we are if we're going to be healed by God. We must be honest about the darker sides of our hearts so we can lay them bare for God to heal. It does no good to pretend we are not a paradox. And why should we? God doesn't want our perfection but simply our broken and contrite hearts. He knows we are filled with both good and bad. We don't have to be afraid to show Him who we truly are. If we want to savor His grace, we must present the sides of ourselves that need His grace! Embracing and sharing the dark nights of my soul is how God's goodness defines and transforms me.

We can also trust God through the bad things other people have done to us. For a lot of people, believing in a good God is hard not because of things they have done but because of the things that were done to them. We live in a world darkened by sin, and there is tremendous suffering that can easily make us cynical about God.

I've seen the darkness, but I still believe in the light. I want to tell you about that now. This personal story includes terrible sexual violence—if you're not in the right place to read this, please skip down to the "Reach Out" section.

In the Midst of Our Pain

When I was nine years old, I was the victim of physical and sexual abuse. A high school student forced me to watch him rape another teenager. It was the most awful experience. He told me to "Sit still and be a man." He was arrested a few days later for his heinous crime against that young woman. Years later, when my brother and I shared an apartment, gang members broke in and pistol-whipped my brother. I was struck over the head repeatedly with a baseball bat. We were both rushed to the hospital with broken bones and busted-up faces. And I've already told you about the time I was shot. I've seen a bit of the darker belly of humanity.

I'm thirty-three now, married to the most beautiful and supportive woman on the planet and father to three amazing children. I have more than I could have ever dreamed of! And yet I still struggle with the dark events of my past. These dark memories still rise up and disturb me on a deep level. Sometimes I wonder, *Why me, God? It's not fair.* Other times I feel at peace and desire reconciliation with every person who ever hurt me. I'll even find myself searching for them on social media. Again, the paradox of my inner self returns. I simultaneously want these men to be blessed and to be thrown in jail. Life is confusing. And the struggle to forgive isn't the whole of it. Sometimes I'm straight-up afraid that someone else will attack me. If I'm alone at a gas station or someplace like that, I'm looking over my shoulder. I can't help it.

Lately, however, God has given me a word that's been helping. Through prayer, He said, *Rashawn, you've allowed the presence of evil men to become larger than the God you profess to serve.* That cut my heart deeply—because it was true. I was allowing my abusers to be larger than God in my life, even as I preached Jesus's words, "Do not fear those who kill the body but cannot kill the soul. But rather fear Him who is able to destroy both soul and body in hell"(Matt. 10:28 NKJV). Ouch and okay, Lord!

I was allowing the fear of men to dominate my life instead of embracing the infinite goodness of the omniscient, omnipotent God.

I'll never know why God allowed certain people to hurt me. And I'll never know exactly why He allowed me to hurt other people too. What I do know is that He remains good through it all. Even though some days are harder than others and the darkness looms large, I take hope from John's Gospel. There is a light shining in the darkness that cannot be overcome by the dark (John 1:5). The people of my past certainly have haunted me, but they won't any longer. May our confidence in God surpass any fear of humankind. I won't fear people, only God. May we say with confidence, "The Lord is my helper; I will not be afraid. What can mere mortals do to me?" (Heb. 13:6).

Through looking back through the experiences in my own life as well as examining the Scriptures, I have discovered a few perks of pain that may benefit you. Pain:

promotes the progress of the gospel.

points us toward God's presence and our purpose.

provides opportunities for us to witness about Jesus.

produces courage in our faith communities to vulnerably share our pain.

proves the character of our relationships.

provokes maturity in our lives.

purifies the motives of our hearts.

prepares us to see life and death in a proper perspective.

That being said, just know when you leave your pain in the loving hands of your perfect heavenly Father, it is never in vain.

START with SUFFERING, END with GOODNESS

"For [Christ] I have *suffered* the loss of all things and count them as rubbish, in order that I may *gain* Christ" (Phil. 3:8 NKJV, emphasis added).

⊕ REACH OUT

Uncover your eyes so you can see how beautiful, powerful, and lovely your Creator truly is. He created the heavens and the earth and everything in them. He made all things. Not only that, He made us in His image to go out and spread His goodness into a world that has fallen away from its original goodness. It's critical for us to understand that God didn't save us from something but made and saved us *for* something.

God's good plan for our lives is not just that we will escape a fallen world but that we will infect this fallen world with His goodness. Make no mistake: our lives, no matter how we choose to live them, will affect others. Nobody's life is totally insulated. That means our influence will either be one that is godly and good or one that is less so.

I recently read about a town in California called Carpinteria. It's one of those places we all long to live: on the Pacific coast, buttressed against mountains, with a laid-back California attitude. But a recent legal change has made the residents of Carpinteria a little less laid-back. With the legalization of marijuana, so many people are growing the plant that beautiful Carpinteria stinks of weed. No matter what the people who live there try to do, they can't escape the smell. It's not the salt spray of the Pacific Ocean you can't get away from; it's the controversial smell of weed.

When I read that, I couldn't help but think about how God calls us to carry His goodness into the world. If we focus on the darker sides of our lives, then that's what's going to come out—and it's going to stink. But if we allow God's goodness to permeate our souls, then His goodness is what will naturally flow out, blessing everyone around us. In essence, we've been *filled* with the immeasurable riches of His glory for one purpose: to be *spilled*.

The goodness of God transcends the tragedies of this fallen world. His goodness declares that everything is a precious gift from Him. James 1:17 says, "Every good and perfect gift is from above, coming down from the Father of the heavenly lights, who does not change like shifting shadows."

Everything you've done that's good.

Everything you've seen that's good.

Everything you've touched that's good.

Everything you've tasted that's good.

Everything you have that's good.

Everything inside you that's good.

Everything you are becoming that's good.

Everything good in your life wasn't given to you because you deserved it but simply because God is good. This is the message our world desperately needs to hear!

This is my deepest awareness of God's goodness: He is always faithful to deliver not what I desire but what I need. Sometimes what I desire is an easier life or a less painful past. At the end of the day, however, I take comfort in the reality that God is good. Because of that, I can trust that all will be well.

TAKING THE NEXT STEP

PAUSE AND PONDER

God didn't have to make everything He created good;
everything He created was good because He created it.

PRESS INTO PRAYER

This goodness gives us the power to believe when others
deny.

This goodness gives us the courage to share Jesus while
others stare.

This goodness gives us the insight to love deeply where
others are painfully wounded.

This goodness gives us joy amid mourning.

Lord,

We long to be more aware of Your presence. Help us to experience the glory of Your goodness. It is in Your goodness we find ourselves resting when we're in Your presence. You have shown Your faithfulness countless times. May we continue to trust in Your goodness and not in our own. I pray that today we will be filled with more of You and less of us.

PROVE TO BE A PRACTICAL PIONEER

Who is a person you could go share God's goodness with right now? Find a friend or stranger who is in need—and fulfill that need for them with great joy. Live your life as a celebration of God's goodness today!

11

Love

I used to want to fix people, but now I just want to be with them.

BOB GOFF

Love is patient, love is kind. It does not envy, it does not boast, it is not proud. It does not dishonor others, it is not self-seeking, it is not easily angered, it keeps no record of wrongs.

1 CORINTHIANS 13:4-5

⬆ COME UP

I hit my knees in prayer one morning in the dingy basement of the Oklahoma County Jail, where I worked. I prayed for the inmates, asking God to guide me and strengthen me to do His will that day. Then I got going on the push-ups, pumping hard until my muscles flared enough that they'd catch the respect of the inmates.

I wasn't trying to show off but rather follow Paul's advice. Paul said, "I have become all things to all people so that by all possible means I might save some" (1 Cor. 9:22–23). Trust me, if you want any respect in a prison, you'd better be able to lift some steel. So that's what I did. When I finished my push-ups, I still had a little downtime before my shift began. As I sat there, relaxing, I felt a strong word of God come upon me. He wasn't calling me to be just polite today—I mean, He wasn't saying I couldn't wear my smile, only that it wasn't going to be enough today. He had a mission for me.

The Holy Spirit was going to direct me toward a specific action. I didn't know what it was going to be, but I needed to commit to it—no matter what. "Yes, Lord," I said. "Whatever You have for me today, I'll do." After that prayer, my mission directives took shape quickly. Be careful what you pray for. We serve a God who listens and replies!

First, I was to rip twenty sheets of printer paper down the middle, and then do it two more times until I had eighty pieces of paper. So I did it. Then God told me to write a personal note on each paper with a single Bible verse to accompany my words. I did that too, although my fingers almost fell off in the process. Who uses pen and paper anymore? Then came the kicker. God asked me to deliver these notes, floor by floor, cell by cell, sharing the gospel of Jesus as I did it. Writing the notes was one thing, but taking them to the prisoners was a whole other level. I got back down on my knees. But God was clear. This was what I needed to do. So I got moving, God leading me through each floor, cell by cell, delivering His good news.

Everything was going well, the Spirit moving powerfully, until I made it to the cells that were segregated from the rest of the jail. These were the guys who had to be removed from the general population due to disciplinary issues. The tough guys. If I was going to run into any trouble, it was going to be here, with these inmates. Time for more prayer. "God," I said, "are You sure You want me to do this?" He confirmed that He did.

I made it to cell 12. The guy in this cell was infamous for being a brawler. Let's call him Shorty. Shorty not only had a reputation in the jail, but he also had what we call "stripes" on the streets. You don't even want to know what that means. Simply put, you didn't want to mess with this guy. I was nervous as I approached his cell, especially because he had, several times before, managed to rig his door and escape at will.

When I got close, I started saying something similar to what I'd been saying all morning, talking about God's love and hope and grace. Just as I was asking if I could pray for him, Shorty cut me off. "Yo, Copeland," he said. "Go grab that book for me, wouldja?" He pointed to a dark book lying on a table in a common area that could be seen from his cell and many others.

"For sure," I said, hustling over to grab the book. I picked it up and saw that it was the Quran. I didn't know him to be a religious man and so I couldn't help but feel the request was his way of mocking my efforts of Christian evangelism. Nevertheless, I walked the book back over to his cell, then pulled the key off my belt and unlocked his meal tray door. I leaned down to open the tray door and give him the book—and warm liquid hit me squarely in the face. The taste and stench of urine in my mouth was overwhelming. I stumbled backward in disbelief. The roar of inmate laughter was all I could hear. I'm talking hundreds of men, all hooting and hollering at the idiot guard who fell for the prank of the century.

They called me Mr. Pisspot, they called me Dummy, and they called me other names I can't recount here. Heat rose from my stomach into my face. I wanted to open that cell door and teach the fool a lesson. I was humiliated and raging inside. How had this day gone from supreme joy to utter misery in a matter of seconds? I had to make a decision about how I'd respond—and I had to do it fast. Hundreds of inmates were watching me. What was the evangelist prison guard going to do to the guy who poured urine in his face? All eyes were on me.

Instead of standing firm and continuing to speak a word of truth in love to Shorty, I turned around and walked immediately toward the elevator, retreating from the segregated population that was still hollering after me. Within seconds I was back in the basement, peeling off my dirty clothes and cleaning myself up in the bathroom. Furiously, I told my supervisor what happened, and I quit my job.

A few minutes after that I was in my car, pulling away from the jail, angry at God for allowing my obedience to have such a disastrous result. And then God spoke to me again.

My day at the jail was far from over.

GO IN

Popular culture is obsessed with love. Turn on the radio. Watch a Netflix show. Almost every song and story is about love. And yet loneliness, divorce, and countless forms of broken relationships run rampant in our society. How can we be so interested in love while also being so awful at practicing it?

Maybe it's because we rarely take time to learn what true love means. I went to some incredible schools, but not one of them even tried to explain love to me. So I went looking for answers on TV from folks like Oprah and Dr. Phil, but their definitions never seemed quite right or big enough. So then I tried coming up with my own definition through my own experiences, but you know how that goes. I made a mess of love. I looked to my friends, but they were really no different. It was almost like everyone around me was confused by love. You know the stories . . .

The friend who sacrifices everything to be with the woman he loves, only that woman isn't his wife.

The bruised wife who begs her abusive husband to stay.

The young girl whose day is completely destroyed because the boy didn't like her Insta post.

The soldier who returns from war only to find his wife in bed with another man.

Love is a war zone with countless casualties. And yet all of us enter the fray. More than anything in life, we want to love someone and have them love us back. It's universal. Why, then, does it cause so much pain? Because we either don't know what love is or we settle for a version of love that is nowhere near what God intended for us to experience. We don't need to hear the latest pop song or see the newest movie to understand what love is all about. All we have to do is look to Jesus.

In Jesus we see the fullness of God's love in the flesh. On Christmas Eve we celebrate the most courageous act in the history of creation: God choosing to strip away every ounce of power and protection and privilege to become the most helpless and vulnerable creature in the world: a baby.

God was no longer content to have His love communicated through prophets and priests. He needed to tell us Himself. He could have done that any way He wanted. *This* is what He chose. Would you be willing to let down every defense, cede all strength, and offer yourself to the world in a state of total vulnerability?

I don't think I would, but God did. Which makes us ask: What kind of God is this?

The kind who wanted you to know who you truly are. A God who won't let you forget your identity. You are so valuable that God will do anything for you to know it. He will stop at no boundary, be thwarted by no attack, and be afraid of no enemy, not even death itself. God chose death so He could save us from death. That's what true love is. "Greater love has no one than this: to lay down one's life for one's friends" (John 15:13). God came into a war zone to save us, the kind of war zone most of us can only imagine.

Aleppo is a city in Syria that has been under siege for more than five years. If you've seen images of it on the news, it basically resembles hell on earth. The destruction is almost unfathomable. In the middle of this hell, however, there is a bright light, a volunteer group of men and women called the White Helmets. Here's what they do.

When an air strike destroys a building or a home, the White Helmets rush into the rubble, unarmed, with only one purpose: to rescue those who have been buried alive. They literally drop to their knees and dig frantically with their hands to save people. Now, here's where it gets dicey: the people dropping the bombs know the White Helmets will do this. And they know the White Helmets will return no fire. So the plane will hang around until the White Helmets appear, then hit them again. This means every time the White Helmets get the call, they know this could be the end. And still, they rush to save. It's an unthinkable act of bravery. It is total vulnerability.

I remember reading an article in which the reporter asked one of the White Helmets how he did it—how he could summon such courage. "I think of one thing," he said. "I want the people under the rubble to know they are not alone."

We talk a lot about love in our culture. But that's what real love looks like.

Over the past few years, many White Helmets have died. But they've saved seventy *thousand* people! Seventy thousand people have been raised to life by their unthinkable acts of bravery. What kind of people would do such a thing? The kind who will stop at nothing to communicate love.

That sounds a lot like a God I know. A God who took any measure—no matter how dangerous and unthinkable—so we may know His love.

To really know the love of Jesus, we have to move beyond knowledge. It's not enough to know about Jesus. We have to actually know Him personally if we want to know His love. You can go to church every Sunday. You can watch every sermon online. You can listen to every podcast about love. You can lead a Bible study. You can even get a PhD—but it all means nothing if you don't know Him personally.

Knowledge about Jesus is helpful and necessary, but it's not enough. We need to know what He did and said. We need to study His life. What matters most, however, is that we know Him in the here and now so we can experience Him. Think of it this way. I can become an expert on Martin Luther King Jr. and know everything there is to know about him. But I can never know Martin Luther King Jr., because he's dead. With Jesus, we can both know about Him and know Him, because He is alive.

Once we come to know Him, we can trust Him with our whole hearts, which in turn allows Him to flood our hearts with love. Unlike our other relationships, we can completely trust Jesus with our hearts. What are you waiting for? Allow yourself to intimately know the greatest Love of all time.

Back to Jail

Even as I pulled out of the jail's parking lot, I knew I wasn't obeying God. The Spirit was clear. If I didn't return, I'd be disobeying God and failing to do what He wanted me to do: share His love with a man who poured urine on me.

In blind obedience, I turned the car around.

Back at the jail, I went straight to the basement to throw on a clean uniform. God continued speaking clearly to me, giving me the confidence I needed to return to the segregated inmates. I didn't want to do it, but I knew I had to. God gave me a mission. I trusted He'd give me everything I needed to succeed.

When I got back to Shorty's floor, the inmates yelled at me. Mr. Pisspot was back for more! Laughter took over the whole floor. I walked straight toward Shorty's cell. As I got closer I saw his smile. "Well, well," he said. "I never would have guessed it. What you gonna do, homie? You come back for more?"

When I got to his cell, I said, "Hey, bro. I'm not here to punish you or fight with you. I'm here to enlighten you with a few true words."

"Oh yeah, what's that?"

"I forgive you, Shorty," I said. "But the really good news isn't that I forgive you but that Jesus forgives you. Not only that, Jesus loves you like crazy. He told me to tell you that. He loves you so much. He hasn't forgotten you. He hasn't given up on you. He has a huge plan for your life."

Shorty said nothing in reply. He just stared at me, smiling from ear to ear as if he hadn't even heard my words. I turned and walked back toward the elevator, moving past all the hooting and hollering. Just before I stepped into the elevator, I heard Shorty's voice rise above the others. "Hey, Copeland! Copeland! Come back! Come back!"

Seriously, God? I thought. *Can't I just go down the elevator and be done with this situation?* Moved again by the Holy Spirit, I left the elevator and walked back to Shorty once more, enduring a fresh onslaught of name-calling.

When I got to the cell, I couldn't believe what I saw. Shorty was crying his eyes out. He put his head up against the cell door window and cried, "I can't even get my own mother to tell me she loves me. You're saying God loves me? Is that true? Can you prove it to me?"

Astonished, I managed to say, "Yes . . . uh, yes I can. Shorty, listen to me. This truth is stronger than the steel doors separating us." I pulled my little Bible out of my back pocket, turned to Psalm 34:18, and read aloud: "The LORD is close to the brokenhearted; he rescues those whose spirits are crushed" (NLT).

Shorty then asked me if I'd come back when my shift was over so we could talk more about Jesus. I told him there was no need to wait. I didn't even bother going downstairs to clock out. Instead, I stayed at his cell, talking, crying, and laughing for hours. We got drunk on the Holy Spirit that night, reading the Bible, even chanting some passages of Scripture together. Eventually, the night shift manager came over to tell me I had to leave, but before I did, Shorty prayed to accept Jesus as his personal Lord and Savior. He asked God to forgive his sin, and he surrendered his life to the Lord. It was miraculous to see the Lord move so swiftly in Shorty's life!

After that, he replaced his reading of the Quran with reading the Gospel of John. Not long after this, Shorty was acquitted of all charges and released from jail. Today he is a preacher on the south side of Oklahoma City.

Right there in the county jail, True Love met Shorty and changed his life forever.

There is no mess God's love won't enter.

True love never sidesteps brokenness. This may be shocking, but hate didn't cause the messiest massacre in history. Angry men didn't put Jesus on the cross. Love did. The bloodstained cross is the canvas on which God paints His story of great mercy, radical love, and miraculous redemption. Did we deserve it? Not at all. We should do the same for other people, like Shorty. Don't carve people out of your life who you feel don't deserve your time. Make every moment an opportunity to share Jesus. People are starving for a love that's true. Share Jesus by becoming love! No matter how terrible or wonderful the circumstances are. We may be known by our performance, or by what we know, but we will always be remembered by our availability and vulnerability to speak His love message into the anguished hearts of others.

You may be wrestling with the idea—you may be thinking, *Could I become love?* Just like Jesus. Beloved, I want to remind you that sharing God's love is attainable if His Spirit is residing in you. The tough path of love has been made easy to access even in the middle of our messy, real-life relationships in this broken world.

We have several ways we can start becoming love right now.

1. Be approachable—not timid. Move out of our cozy comfort zone.
2. Be full of grace—not judgmental. Live in grace and never limit our love for people we think don't deserve it.
3. Be fierce—not fearful. Always speak the truth in love regardless of potential rejection.

4. Be sacrificial—not selfish. The greatest way to tell if our love tank is empty is if we are failing to show empathy. We must empty ourselves of ourselves for the sake of empathy.

5. Be mindful—not indifferent. Be intentional about seeing what others don't.

Consider which one of these five things you could work on to love more like Jesus. Which one is the easiest for you? Which one is the toughest? Take a moment and think about your personal relationships. Who has been that sharp thorn in your side lately? Is it your coworker, your friend, your spouse, or your nagging landlord? I don't want you to think I'm telling you to stand up and confess that you hate anyone. I just want you to think about how much more they need to experience God's love through you. Jesus empowers us to graciously shower others with the love we never deserved ourselves.

God is love, and that means you are loved to love the hurtful.

God is light, and His light lives in you so you can shine it in a dark world.

God is enough, and you are filled with His enough-ness to fill up empty hearts.

God is who He says He is, and He made you His beloved to be devoted to serving the broken.

TAKING THE NEXT STEP

PAUSE AND PONDER

God's love gladly chases us down until we are found. As you read this, Jesus is meeting you right where you are—mess and all. There is no mess His love won't enter. That includes yours!

PRESS INTO PRAYER

Lord,

Thank You for reassuring me daily that You love me like crazy. I'm in awe of how You are the definition of love even when I fail to believe it. I fully lay my at-times-unlovable life in Your hands. When I do, Love continues to provide where I lack. Love continues to make sure I'm taken care of. I'm forever thankful for Love showing up for me and embracing me regardless of my mess. Grace will always be enough. You see me for me. I'm insanely imperfect, yet You still love me.

PROVE TO BE A PRACTICAL PIONEER

We must stop begging for scraps of fickle love. When we live from a deep assurance that we are fully loved by God, we won't find ourselves anxious for temporal love. Let's live loved today so we can *be* love today. Go remind a friend Who love is . . .

12

Start Where You Are but Don't Look Back

If you cling to your life, you will lose it, and if you let your life go, you will save it.

LUKE 17:33 NLT

A life totally committed to God has nothing to fear, nothing to lose, nothing to regret.

PANDITA RAMABAI (1858–1922)

COME UP

A Christian's goal is not to live long but to live well. Our call is not to extend our days but to live our days according to the purposes of God, seizing each moment for His glory and the advancement of His kingdom. We cannot serve two masters (Matt. 6:24). We either pursue our own glory or the glory of the One. Getting the most out of life isn't about what we do or what we have, even though the world says otherwise. When was the last time you went to a party and someone didn't ask what you did for a living? When was the last time you weren't judged for the car you drive or the shoes you wear?

This world is intensely focused on doing *stuff* and having *things*. It starts in elementary school, when we ask children what they want to be when they grow up, and crescendos with the never-ending parade during senior year of high school. There's always that next thing to do or that new thing to become. When we allow our lives to become nothing more than the progression up the ladder of success, we rob ourselves of the deep meaning God intends for our lives. Instead of growing in love and maturity, we grow stressed, oppressed, and depressed.

We were made for so much more. The great thing about being a Christian is that we don't have to wonder what we should do with our lives. The Bible tells us. We bring God glory by conforming our lives to the life of Christ in a pattern of self-sacrificial love. This means we love our neighbors as ourselves. This requires a divinely empowered, self-sacrificial life. So let's take a moment to learn more about God's own sacrificial nature.

Remember the story of Noah's ark? God un-creates the world of Eden with a great flood, preserving only a remnant of His original creation with Noah and his family on the ark. Then God reestablishes the world with the first biblical covenant: He promises to never destroy the world that way again. A little review of something we covered earlier in this book might be helpful. At creation God deemed all of creation good, but we insisted on corrupting it through violent sin. God, grieving over the ruined original creation, resolved to destroy those who had done the destroying. I know that's hard to hear. Every time I read it, I think, *Really, God? I mean, we humans lose our tempers, but aren't You supposed to keep it together and all that?*

Thinking about God taking such violent action is especially difficult these days with all the violence going on in the world: wars, mass shootings, suicides. But this story *is* in the Bible, which means it's true and teaches us something important about God. But what can we learn from a story where God drowns His good earth, rescues only a few, and gives them another chance sealed with a covenant?

The covenant part of the story is important. Think of it as a divine response to a theological paradox: God has a desperate need to create a peaceful world. If He is going to create something, then it must be peaceful. But God also has a desperate need to be compassionate to people who insist on disrupting the peace. See the pickle God is in?

A quick word about *covenant*, because you may be wondering what that word even means. A covenant clarifies a legal situation by providing new legal grounding between partners. In this covenant, God commits to new rules with humanity. The covenant requires nothing of us. It sets limits only upon God. God promises never to flood the world again. Noah doesn't promise anything. To seal His promise, God sets His rainbow in the sky.

So what do we learn? We learn that God loves us so much, He's willing to change. Christian redemption is a mutable humanity being fit to an immutable God. The God of this covenant is unchanging, sure, but only in His refusal to give up on us. God chooses to limit Himself because His heart is grieved by our suffering. The God declaring this covenant is not an objective judge meting out a just sentence but a lover who does anything to reconcile with His beloved. We serve a God of reconciliation, not judgment.

We also learn that God isn't angry. In this story, God becomes not only our Creator but also our Protector. He hangs His bow in the sky as a sign of that promise. In the ancient world, lightning was seen as arrows flung by God's mighty bow. The rainbow reminds us that God will never again take up the divine bow against us.

Finally, we see God's willingness to sacrifice His own freedom, foreshadowing the passion of Jesus Christ on the cross. God wanted communion with us so badly that He was willing to send His Son as one of us to die for us so we could be reunited in everlasting life. From the very beginning of Genesis until Revelation, the Bible reveals a God willing to sacrifice His own freedoms for the sake of His beloved.

⊙ GO IN

No Moment Wasted

Each moment of our lives is sacred and of value. Each can be redeemed and used for God's purposes. Viewing life through this lens helps us understand there are no throwaway moments. All that is required of us is that we place God at the center of our lives. Then we experience the more we were created for. This reorientation takes daily, moment-by-moment decision.

I'm reminded of a commonly told story I once heard about Pablo Picasso sitting in a Paris café. An admirer walked up and asked him to make a quick sketch on a paper napkin. Picasso agreed, drew a dove, and handed it back to the admirer. Picasso then requested a huge amount of money for his work. Taken aback, the admirer said, "How can you ask for so much? It took you a minute to draw this." To which Picasso replied, "No, it took me forty years."

Picasso understood the value of each moment of life. There isn't a single moment that doesn't matter. His ability to draw that dove in a matter of seconds could not be separated from the years of preparation that had come before it. Life isn't spread out in separate episodes like some type of television series. All of the sacrifices we've made and haven't made play a part in who we are and what we're able to do now. This includes the tragedies and mistakes that may currently be keeping us from facing our future.

I'm not saying we're a sum total of what we've done. We are not, as so many believe, only what happened to us. Our lives are not determined by our past but how we view our past. When we think of our past, we should see it as a great reference point but a terrible residence. Don't live there. The thoughts we allow to nest in our minds will eventually be our actions. Negative thoughts produce negative habits. Christlike thoughts produce Christlike lives. Put simply: we become whatever we do.

Think about NBA All-Star Stephen Curry. Nobody expected him to be the kind of player he is today. He didn't receive a scholarship to the school of his dreams, Virginia Tech, where his dad had been a star. Instead, he walked on at Davidson College, a school with considerably less athletic prestige. Instead of moping about it, Curry dedicated himself to becoming the best player he could be. He was small, unheralded, and played for a team that was regularly overlooked. Back then, it would have been impossible to predict Curry would or could become the superstar he is today. But he understood he could rise above his humble beginnings by maximizing each moment he was given. So that's what he did. He practiced relentlessly and took advantage of every single moment. And the rest, as they say, is history.

Our lives are comprised of small moments, individual decisions where we choose either to sacrifice or indulge and then experience the corresponding loss or reward. We reap what we sow (Gal. 6:7). So the question of what we are sowing, moment by moment, day by day, becomes crucial—especially in light of eternity.

We must radically commit ourselves to sowing eternal seeds, whether we feel like they are small or not. There's nothing small about sowing "in sacrifice." Especially if it's eternal. There's great hope in the harvest of heaven. After all, Jesus said that if we have faith as small as a mustard seed, we can move mountains (Matt. 17:20).

We must die to ourselves moment by moment, day by day, in order to bear much fruit. Eternity will be filled with the harvest we commit our lives to sowing. We are the essential workers of God's kingdom, planting seeds where people need it most.

Becoming Like Christ Today

Christlikeness is not self-improvement but self-expenditure. It's not what we gain but what Jesus pours into and out of us that counts most. Jesus said, "He who believes in Me, as the Scripture has said, out of his heart will flow rivers of living water" (John 7:38 NKJV). It is not the will of God to make us beautifully rounded grapes only for display, but it is His delight to squish the sweetness out of us so we become channels of His blessings to others. Our lives are a sacrifice. To sacrifice is to relinquish or to resign ourselves to someone or something beyond ourselves. In other words, it is an offering prompted by love for the object of our adoration.

There is perhaps no better embodiment of this kind of self-sacrifice (other than Jesus Himself) than the woman who crashed one of Jesus's dinner parties. Here's what happened: Jesus and the disciples are having dinner, when a woman, uninvited, appears. In her hands is an alabaster jar filled with nard, which was ridiculously expensive perfume. By some accounts, the amount she had with her would have equated to an entire year's wages. The woman takes the jar, breaks it open, and pours the perfume on Jesus's head, anointing him (Mark 14:3). The disciples are furious at the impractical offering. Jesus, however, praises her. He delights in her elaborate showcase of love. She could have, no doubt, used this oil for her own benefit, but instead chose to give it all to Jesus in an expression of love for Him.

If our love does not carry us beyond ourselves, it is not a truly self-sacrificial love. As Christians, our love cannot always be sensible and discreet; sometimes it should be filled with abandon. Christian love does not calculate but gives away all without delay. The Good Samaritan didn't stop to consider whether or not the man lying half-dead in the road was a good man. All he saw was a person who needed help and so he offered help, no questions asked. This is the kind of love Jesus displayed on the cross and the kind He calls us to today.

Have you ever been carried away to do something for God, not because it was a good idea but simply out of your great love for God and His desire that you totally abandon yourself to Him? God calls us to live sold out, seeing each moment as an opportunity not to protect ourselves but to serve Him with total faith that He'll provide for our needs.

I have the privilege of working for one of the fastest-growing Christian organizations, led by Craig Groeschel of Life.Church. When I visit the central offices for my quarterly meetings, I'm inspired by the words we have plastered on the walls. They serve as a reminder to each staff member every single day that they are called to be "Faith-filled, big-thinking, bet-the-farm risk takers. We'll never insult God with small thinking and safe living."

It's important to constantly remind ourselves we are called to be brave for Christ. Will we risk everything—our comfort, our possessions, our security, our safety, even our very lives—to reach a dark and dying world with the light of Jesus Christ? The moment we sit back and wait for a tingly feeling or the perfect time, it will be too late. Let's start here, and right now. *We have no time to waste.* There is no better moment than now to make the bold decision to rise up and take whatever risk to radically live for God.

We can't waste our lives sitting in the comfort zone. We must stand up and let our lights shine for the billions of people who are headed toward a Christless eternity.

REACH OUT

Finding Light in Sacrifice

You don't have to go on a mission trip to be on mission for Jesus. You aren't just needed overseas; you're needed right across the street. There are people in your school, your family, even your church, who need Jesus. They're waiting for you—in your local grocery store, homeless shelter, and mall. You can shine a self-sacrificial light today. There's no reason to wait!

In the Gospel of Matthew, Jesus says, "Let your light shine before men, that they may see your good works and glorify your Father in heaven" (Matt. 5:16 NKJV). Jesus isn't just compelling us to do good works. He *assumes* we will do good works. He's not saying, "Slow down from your busy lives and get a life coach to motivate you into the next big thing." He's pleading with us to lay

START with COMFORT, END with COMMITMENT

down our lives, abide in Him, and allow the Holy Spirit to produce good works in us right where we are, right now. Good works will be the natural result of a life lived with Jesus. "I am the vine; you are the branches. If you remain in me and I in you, you will bear much fruit; apart from me you can do nothing" (John 15:5).

But we have to remember that mission work is not the ultimate goal of the church. Worship is. God is clamoring for your *heart* long before He's pleading for your *hand*. Missions exist because worship isn't everywhere. We must open our hearts, sit before Him expectantly, and fully surrender to Him before He will greatly use us. We must abide in God before we attempt to revive anyone else. A once-dim heart becomes lit and ready for service only after authentic worship. It is genuine worship that produces good works. If we aren't producing the good works for Jesus, then we have to examine what is holding us back.

What held Jesus back from producing good works for God the Father? *Nothing at all.* His birthday serves as a reminder of how He gave Himself up for others, including me and you. His concerns were often overlooked and unnoted. We typically love to be celebrated and receive countless amounts of attention. Our birthdays are always about us. But Jesus gave up heavenly royalty to come down to earthly poverty to be with us in this mess we made. Jesus spent every day pouring Himself out for people who rarely would pour into Him. He emptied Himself so we could be filled with the light of sacrifice.

Darkness cannot put out the Light—but that doesn't mean it won't try. Darkness always opposes God's plan for our lives. God's Word helps light the path for His perfect plan for your life. He wants your light to shine. The world, however, wants to hide your light. But the words of Jesus continue to encourage us to let it shine despite opposition. Jesus said, "No one lights a lamp and then puts it under a basket. Instead, a lamp is placed on a stand, where it gives light to everyone in the house" (Matt. 5:15 NLT).

Even on our messy days, we are God's love letter to the world, "written not with ink but with the Spirit of the living God" (1 Cor. 3:3). We are set apart to not only communicate but to demonstrate His glory to a messy and dying world. Allow your light to shine even through the dark cracks of your own heart.

Popular advice in today's culture I can't find in Scripture:

1. Do what makes you happy.
2. Create the life you want.
3. Love yourself first.
4. Follow your heart.

The truth about sacrifice we're called to as believers according to God's Word:

1. Offer yourself as a living sacrifice (Rom. 12:1).
2. Seek first the kingdom of God (Matt. 6:33).
3. Love the Lord your God with all your heart, soul, strength, and mind (Luke 10:27).
4. Deny yourself, take up your cross, and follow Christ (Luke 9:23).

Don't Look Back

The spiritual journey is rarely clean. A mess inevitably awaits us around each corner. We all fall. We all falter. We all fail. We don't know how or when trial will come, only that it will. When it does, there will be temptation to turn away from God and back to relying on our own sinful nature. When this happens, we must remember the choice we made to follow Jesus. It is a choice that must be remade every single day. Will we focus on Christ or our old way of life? Will we stay down in the dirt or stand up in delight for God?

Do you remember what happened to Lot's wife in Genesis 19? She lived in Sodom, a city famous for its sexual sin. To escape its destruction, she had to be dragged out of the town. On the way out of town, she looked back and was instantly turned into a pillar of salt (v. 26). It's kind of a weird story. The Hebrew words used to describe this "looking back" imply that she didn't really want to leave her past behind. Even though God was literally destroying it, she still longed for it.

Our pasts are hard to abandon. Sodom was where her memories lived. Everything she knew was there. Even though the city was deeply sinful, it was *her* city, and she longed for it. She chose her past over and above her future. Instead of embracing the freedom God had for her in the future, she remained trapped in the sin of her past. And so she lost her life. The message of the story is clear: living like that only leads to death.

Hear Jesus calling out to you today to not look back.

Don't go back for the money.
Don't go back for the ex.
Don't go back for the drugs.
Don't go back for the fame.
Don't go back for the power.
Joyfully leave what's familiar for the unknown. Move forward by faith into the future I have for you.

God longs to guide you into the freedom- and purpose-filled future He has for you. Don't look back over your shoulder at the allure of your past. God's eyes are always gazing at our hearts to see where they are fixed. He wants our character and our focus to be aimed at knowing Him and becoming more like Him, not our messy pasts.

Started an Orphan, Ending as a Son

I jumped off the jam-packed elevator at Mercy Hospital with my two children, Jerrell and Aiden, eager to introduce them to their newest sibling, our baby Eliyah. I asked Jerrell if he thought Eliyah looked more like me or Denisse. He said neither. "More like Mr. Potato Head!" *Thanks, Jerrell.*

Later in the day, some friends of ours came by for a visit with their six-year-old daughter. She was totally into the baby, rubbing his oily hair and smiling from ear to ear. She touched his little fingers, inspected his feet, and adored his little ears. Then she looked up at me and Denisse and, pointing at the identification bracelet around his tiny ankle, said, "Hey, look, somebody left the price tag on the baby."

How priceless is that comment? Do you know God has placed the most precious price tag on you? We are priceless to Him, today and forever. Unlike my son's "price tag," which had to be removed before we could take him home from the hospital, our price tag from our heavenly Father is never removed.

We are not orphans or slaves to God. We have been adopted by the Father. We are His children (Rom. 8:15)! Children don't have to do anything to earn the love of their parents. They are simply loved for existing. Likewise, you don't have to have it all together to come to God. God loves you right where you are—but He loves you far too much to let you stay there.

No one is ever prepared enough or perfect enough to step into the presence of a holy, loving God. We just have to believe He wants us to do it and then take the leap, with no more feeling afraid and unprepared to step into the future God has planned for us.

So let's do it. Let's start walking right where we are to become more like the person He's always wanted us to be like: Jesus.

TAKING THE NEXT STEP

PAUSE AND PONDER

Whatever shame is keeping you from a fresh start with God, whatever old baggage is dragging you down, whatever broken pieces are in your heart, *start right there*. Yes! Start right there—with God this time.

PRESS INTO PRAYER

Be imitators of God, as beloved children. And walk in love, as Christ loved us and gave himself up for us, a fragrant offering and sacrifice to God. (Eph. 5:1–2 ESV)

Lord,

I thank You for sharing Your unfailing hope and for a fresh start where yesterday's worries aren't being carried into today. I pray that You continue to order my steps and guide my mind. May I surround myself with Your truth. Your Word. Your wisdom. Your love. Your peace.

PROVE TO BE A PRACTICAL PIONEER

Jesus laid down His life on the cross for us without hesitation. No plan B. No second thoughts. Just as Christ sacrificed Himself for us, we should Reach Out and sacrifice ourselves for others. How can you lay your life down today?

Start.

Start now.

Start where you are.

Start with what you have.

Start with what you don't have.

Start with your fears and your frustrations.

Start with what you don't know and what you do know.

Start moving away from your doubts and toward God.

Start with your mess-ups and knockdowns.

Start small and weak.

Start now.

Just start.

Start where you are, and God will take you where you need to be.

Today Is the Day

This message isn't to turn bad people good. It's to make dead people alive. There are only two groups of people in the world—those who are being saved and those who are perishing. *I say this with tears!*

Jesus said, "He who is not with Me is against Me" (Matt. 12:30 NKJV). No one can inherit God's kingdom by straddling the fence of lukewarm Christianity. Until you place your trust in Jesus Christ alone, you are among the perishing. Jesus also said, "Very truly I tell you, no one can see the kingdom of God unless they are born again" (John 3:3), and His disciple John would later write, "Whoever has the Son has life" (1 John 5:12).

Jesus Is the Way, the Truth, and the Life

If we grasp Jesus's love and embrace His life, we will have life forever. However, if we choose not to run to Jesus, we won't have it. Not now. Not ever. "God has given us eternal life, and this life is in his Son" (v. 11). I can't finish this book without warning you about hell—just as heaven is real, hell is too. But God's mercy is crying out to you, "The Lord is not slow in keeping his promise, as some understand slowness. Instead he is patient with you, not wanting anyone to perish, but everyone to come to repentance" (2 Pet. 3:9).

The apostle Paul wrote, "Behold, now is the day of salvation" (2 Cor. 6:2 ESV). That statement could not be any clearer. The day of salvation is not when you're ready, it's today! Right now. Start here. Jesus is whispering to your heart, "Come to me that you may have life" (John 5:40 ESV). Beloved, if you *start where you are*, you will be truly made alive into who God has called you to be.

The Greatest News Ever

The gospel is the greatest news we'll ever hear. And that news is this: Jesus Christ, the Son of God, accomplished the perfect life we couldn't and died on a cross—became our substitute—to pay the price for all our sins and endure and erase all of God's wrath. Then He rose from the dead! He was victorious over death; the tomb is now empty so we don't have to be. We can enjoy eternal life and freedom in His presence—and all of this is given freely through faith in Jesus Christ alone. That's the gospel. It came at an expensive price we could never afford. Christ paid it for us. For me. For *you*.

Up to this very moment, thousands of years after Jesus "became flesh and blood and moved into the neighborhood" (John 1:14 MSG), there's never been a news station in town able to deliver greater news. And we have strangers across the street and family members across the hall who have not heard this news.

So, here's the point: God met you in your mess so you can go meet others in theirs.

A Closing Prayer

The Salvation Prayer of David (Psalm 51)

Have mercy on me, O God,
    according to your unfailing love;
according to your great compassion
    blot out my transgressions.
Wash away all my iniquity
    and cleanse me from my sin.
For I know my transgressions,
    and my sin is always before me.
Against you, you only, have I sinned
    and done what is evil in your sight;
so you are right in your verdict
    and justified when you judge.
Surely I was sinful at birth,
    sinful from the time my mother conceived me . . .
Cleanse me with hyssop, and I will be clean;
    wash me and I will be whiter than snow . . .
Create in me a pure heart, O God,
    and renew a steadfast spirit within me.
Do not cast me from your presence
    or take your Holy Spirit from me.
Restore to me the joy of your salvation
    and grant me a willing spirit, to sustain me.
Then will I teach transgressors your ways,
    so that sinners will turn back to you. (vv. 1–5, 7,
        10–13)

Shout Out

I would be typing for decades if I were to list all the people who have influenced me and contributed to *Start Where You Are*, yet I can't miss this opportunity to recognize a special few.

For my precious bride. Without your support and encouragement, Denisse, this book would have never seen the light of day. I love sharing this hopeful message alongside you.

For my beautiful family. Jerrell, Aiden, Eliyah, Renea, Rodney, Mashawn, Tuswani, Shamaad, and the rest of my precious family.

For my amazing agent. Words fail to express how fortunate I am to have one of the finest agents under the sun, Amanda Luedeke. She always brings joy into our conversations even when they are tough. Thank you for being a dear friend to our family.

For my good friend Ryan Casey Waller. Thank you for helping to make this book pop, and not only that but also serving as my literary therapist. I'm deeply grateful for your ongoing commitment and priceless contribution.

For my Godsent editors and the rest of the family at Baker Books. Brian Thomasson, guiding light and the vision catcher, gave me room to share the message I was deeply convicted to write about. Thank you for digging deeper, along with senior editor Lindsey Spoolstra and freelance editor Meredith Hinds. Together, you are a dream team—a real force to be reckoned with in the editorial world. The whole team at Baker Books: Patti Brinks, Abby Van Wormer, Eileen Hanson, Olivia Peitsch, Melanie Burkhardt—editors, artists, assistants, receptionists, marketers, and dealmakers—you are the absolute greatest!

I'm humbled to have the opportunity to write a book that will be a breath of fresh air for many who read it. While it's been a tremendous undertaking, it's been invaluable to join arms with the industry's finest.

For my friends through thick and thin:

Al Len. Thank you for loving our family no matter what. Love you, brother.

The Maguires. You are the most loving and supportive family on the face of the planet. You help the Copelands grow, live, and thrive as a family. Thanks for meeting us where we were.

The Lewises. Your unconditional love and encouragement have been at the center of the toughest times we've had. You are much more than friends.

The Sumalpongs. You are such great examples; we enjoy every moment with our I'm So Blessed Daily family.

Bryan. Your endless words of support and affirmation will never be forgotten.

The Daniels. You are the cutest couple in town. We are super excited about your growing family. Thank you for helping us grow as a blended family.

The Coopers. Thank you for planting People's Church and welcoming us home—every Sunday morning.

Matt Brown. You have been a friend, mentor, counselor, and digital discipler. And all of these at once when I needed it the most. Thank you!

Adam Weber. Thank you for always showing me that "Love Has a Name"—Jesus. Embrace Church changed our lives.

Deshon. You have encouraged me more than you'll ever know.

The Stanleys. You are our favorites, and ministry would be so much tougher without you.

The Earps. Thank you for taking a risk on me. You have been a leader I've admired, Steve, and have shown me how to lead from beneath—starting with my wife. Love you and the Elevators!

The Goerings. It's been such an honor to partner with you. You are world changers!

The Ezes. We honor your wisdom and insights daily and are forever grateful to know such a special couple.

The Greys. You are a reflection of Jesus and the church and the most humorous couple we know. We love you.

Darnell. I never met a man who smiles more than me until I met you. Lol!

Roe the Barber. You've given me three years of fresh haircuts and life-giving conversations. You are gifted. Thanks for being my friend.

Rai Willis. You were the beacon of light I needed during my UCO Army ROTC days. God used you to plant seeds that would later flourish.

David Medina. Your story inspires me. Every time I find myself in a ding, I remember the faith and perseverance of your life.

Bobby Gruenewald and the Life.Church family. The day we met I knew you were someone special. Thank you for trusting me enough to allow me to serve next to you. I'm forever grateful to be part of such a great organization.

For you, beloved reader. Thank you for entrusting to me your most valuable asset: your time. This may be the first of my books you've read. (Great to meet you!) If so, I hope this will be the first of many, and I hope you enjoyed it.

For Jesus, the real MVP. I reserve my final salute for You. You know I didn't want to write again. I was insecure because my worth got caught up in the words of a kindergarten teacher who told me to never pick up a pen and write again (and man, that hurt). But thank You for healing and restoring me. You cleansed my heart and gave me a brand-new pen. Jesus, I will forever cling to these truths like the lifeline they are.

Thank You for allowing me to start where I was. You brought me right where I needed to be—with You.

Notes

Chapter 1 From Dirty to Worthy

1. Bob Goff, Facebook post, February 13, 2019, https://www.facebook.com/bob goffis/posts/if-you-think-your-mess-up-is-bigger-than-gods-grace-thats-your -second-mistake/2452181111523814/.

2. Max Lucado, "Do Our Prayers Matter?" *Max Lucado*, accessed February 17, 2020, https://maxlucado.com/listen/do-our-prayers-matter/.

Chapter 2 Where I Started

1. Romans 8:38–39.

Chapter 3 Peace

1. Louie Giglio, Facebook post, May 21, 2019, https://www.facebook.com /officialLouieGiglio/posts/1228807233961984?comment_id=12288276806266 06&comment_tracking=%7B%22tn%22%3A%22R%22%7D.

Chapter 4 Conviction

1. Billy Graham @BillyGraham, Twitter post, June 23, 2016, https://twitter .com/billygraham/status/746096841159217153.

2. Bob Goff @bobgoff, Twitter post, June 5, 2014, https://twitter.com/bobgoff /status/474584993969094656?lang=en.

3. As quoted by Robert Greene, "Robert Greene Quotable Quotes," *Good-reads*, accessed February 18, 2020, https://www.goodreads.com/quotes/73905 16-in-a-speech-abraham-lincoln-delivered-at-the-height-of.

4. David Van Biema, "Mother Teresa's Crisis of Faith," *TIME*, August 23, 2007, https://time.com/4126238/mother-teresas-crisis-of-faith/.

5. Blaise Pascal, *Pensées* (New York: Penguin Books, 1966), 75.

6. Jim Carrey, "Jim Carrey Quotable Quotes," *Goodreads*, accessed February 18, 2020, https://www.goodreads.com/quotes/1151805-i-think-everybody -should-get-rich-and-famous-and-do.

7. Bob Goff @bobgoff, Twitter post, April 17, 2017, https://twitter.com/bob goff/status/853980302057758721?lang=en.

Chapter 6 Patience

1. Alice Walker, *The Color Purple* (Boston: Houghton Mifflin Harcourt, 1982), 91.

Chapter 8 Joy

1. Debra Fileta, *Choosing Marriage: Why It Has to Start with We > Me* (Eugene, OR: Harvest House, 2018), 135.

2. Kay Warren, "Joy Is a Choice You Can Make Today," *Choose Joy: Because Happiness Isn't Enough*, accessed February 19, 2020, http://kaywarren.com /choosejoy/.

3. "Stephen Colbert and Anderson Cooper's Beautiful Conversation about Grief," YouTube video, 21:13, uploaded August 17, 2019, by Mostly Water, https://www.youtube.com/watch?v=YB46h1koicQ.

4. Dietrich Bonhoeffer, *Theological Education Underground: 1937–1940, Dietrich Bonhoeffer Works*, vol. 15, ed. Victoria J. Barnett, trans. Claudia D. Bergmann, Peter Frick, and Scott A. Moore (Minneapolis, MN: Fortress Press, 2011), 5.

5. "April 08 (1945): Anti-Nazi Theologian Dietrich Bonhoeffer Is Hanged," *This Day in History*, accessed February 19, 2020, https://www.history.com/this -day-in-history/defiant-theologian-dietrich-bonhoeffer-is-hanged.

CONNECT WITH
RASHAWN

Jesus was always passionate about people. His greatest ability was His availability. Rashawn is excited to get to know you. He'd love to chat with you! If you want to speak with him, reach out at rashawn@startwhereyouarebook.com.

You can also reach out to him on

 **@hypesir**    **@hypesir7**

Here's his phone number if you'd like to give him a call:
(405) 596-8240

Rashawn is open to visiting your college, conference, church, or audience to host, keynote, or share a message. Rashawn is a minister who writes and a writer who speaks. He has a unique perspective, and he's a passionate storyteller. If you are interested in having Rashawn visit your event, contact rashawn@startwhereyouarebook.com.

Connect with
BakerBooks
Relevant. Intelligent. Engaging.

Sign up for announcements about new and upcoming titles at

BakerBooks.com/SignUp

@ReadBakerBooks